HARDLY WORKING
AT COLLEGE

The Overachieving Underperformer's Guide to Graduating Without Cracking a Book

Written by Chris Morran
Illustrated by Mike Pisiak

SIMON SPOTLIGHT ENTERTAINMENT
New York   London   Toronto   Sydney

SIMON SPOTLIGHT ENTERTAINMENT
An imprint of Simon & Schuster
1230 Avenue of the Americas, New York, New York 10020

An EYE book

Conceived, designed, and produced by
EYE
276 Fifth Avenue
Suite 205
New York, NY 10001

Editorial and Art Direction: Michael Driscoll
Cover and Interior Design: Sheila Hart Design, Inc.
Copyeditor: Jennifer Pricola
Proofreader: Adam Sommers

Publisher: William Kiester

Manufactured in China
First Edition 10 9 8 7 6 5 4 3 2 1

Library of Congress Cataloging-in-Publication Data
Morran, Chris.
Hardly working at college : the overachieving underperformer's guide to graduating without cracking a book /
written by Chris Morran ; illustrated by Mike Pisiak.— 1st ed.
p. cm.
An EYE book
ISBN 1-4169-0660-6
1. College students—Humor. 2. Universities and colleges—Humor. I. Title.
PN6231.C6M67 2005
818'.607—dc22
2005005966

To the memory of Thomas Jefferson,
third president of the United States
and founder of the University of Virginia,
who died penniless so that I could have a place
to hang out between the ages of
eighteen and twenty-two.
Thanks, T.J.!

ACKNOWLEDGMENTS

It's my name on the cover, but there are many people who deserve thanks either for helping with the book, or for putting up with me in general: William Kiester at EYE for making the book a reality; the Hardly Working creative team of Michael Driscoll, Mike Pisiak, and Sheila Hart for making it funnier and more attractive; Meghann Marco for letting me borrow one of her sneakier ideas; Kevin Finn, Chris Garcia, Jessica Anderson, and the rest of my friends from the University who swear they never did any of the things detailed in this book; Ashlie Atkinson, Kim Tracey, Martha Mihalick, Emily Russo, Kris Wilton, Kevin DeBernardi, and everyone at Botanica for giving me something to do on the nights when I didn't feel like writing.

Contents

III: CLASSWORK

IV: HOMEWORK

V: ADVANCED STUDIES

VI: ACADEMIA AD ETERNUM: GRADUATE SCHOOL AND BEYOND

Just how did you end up in this mess? All of your friends were doing it, so you assumed it was safe to try it out for yourself. You thought it would be the perfect escapist trip to stave off the inevitable: the abysmal sink-hole of living responsibly in a civilized society. And besides, it's not like it's your money that's vanished into the unknown with little or nothing to show for it. The thought that all those lurid movies and books might not be telling you the whole truth never crossed your mind. Well, it's too late now; the illusion is beginning to crumble around you. . . and you still have four years of college to go.

The chilling reality of post-adolescent academia is thus: College is a com-plicated maze peopled with bureaucratic administrators (only a bursar knows what a bursar does), grad students who sneer at you for not being as cultured and educated as they are, and professors who require you to memorize (and therefore purchase) their one published book, which they've been able to foist upon the college bookstore. The nightmarish-ness of it all is enough to make even the sturdiest of students long for a return to the simplicity of high school. However, wish though one might, there's no going back to the halcyon days of your teens. Thus, coping mechanisms are required.

Some (rather naïve) students opt to face the collegiate challenges head-on by doing too much. The foolhardy Overachiever spends the majority of his free time studying, actively participating in clubs and student government, and generally finding new ways of minimizing the amount of free time he has. Sure, he graduates with stellar grades and a bloated résumé, but he hasn't truly enjoyed a moment of his past four years; and the truth is, future employers don't care much that he was treasurer of the student council.

The bane of the Overachiever's existence is the Underperformer, who, if she's even managed to work up the energy to fill out an application for college, follows the path of least academic resistance. Of her professors, only the long-haired hippie in the sociology department who sponsors the ultimate frisbee team knows her name. Sure, the Underperformer's college life is nothing but a continuous stream of waking up in strange places just before the sun sets... until the expulsion letter arrives and she suddenly finds herself spending most of her time with her new drinking buddies: Mom and Dad.

There is, of course, another type of student to consider. Her appearance and classroom demeanor reek of grade grubbing; and yet she hasn't been to a class in a week. Every time she asks questions during lecture, she appears to understand exactly what the professor's talking about; and yet, she never seems to take notes. Her grades are better than average, and the faculty all seem to know her on a first-name basis; yet she doesn't study, and her writing is mediocre. Who is she? She's who you'll be when you've finished reading this: an Overachieving Underperformer.

The Overachiever

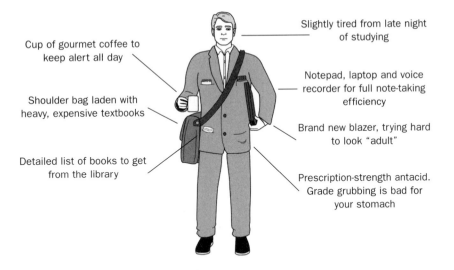

Cup of gourmet coffee to keep alert all day

Shoulder bag laden with heavy, expensive textbooks

Detailed list of books to get from the library

Slightly tired from late night of studying

Notepad, laptop and voice recorder for full note-taking efficiency

Brand new blazer, trying hard to look "adult"

Prescription-strength antacid. Grade grubbing is bad for your stomach

The Underperformer

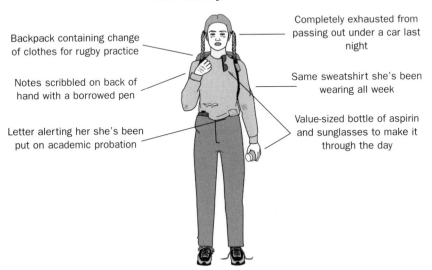

Backpack containing change of clothes for rugby practice

Notes scribbled on back of hand with a borrowed pen

Letter alerting her she's been put on academic probation

Completely exhausted from passing out under a car last night

Same sweatshirt she's been wearing all week

Value-sized bottle of aspirin and sunglasses to make it through the day

The Overachieving Underperformer

Backpack containing only a copy of her history professor's rare book of poetry

Well-rested from her afternoon nap

Black velvet coat to match her English professor

Laptop so she can instant message the cute guy three seats over

Vitamins. She'll need her strength if she intends on skipping her economics class

Glowing letter of recommendation from the toughest professor on campus

Two cups of coffee (and a bearclaw) so she can share with her professor

SECTION I
Orientation

Just as the heart surgeon doesn't make it into the oper-
ating room without first taking a few basic anatomy
classes, so too must the Overachieving Underperformer
begin by mastering the basics—when to skip class,
what to say when you're caught skipping class, where
to sit when you don't skip class—before moving on to
more advanced techniques. The pages that follow serve
as a primer for everyone from the prospective under-
grad looking to find just the right slack-friendly college
to the current college student hoping to brush up on his
or her class-avoidance techniques.

Chapter 1

BEING THE SMARTEST OF THE DUMB KIDS: SELECTING YOUR SCHOOL

Primary to the practice of hardly working your way through college is that you attend college. The good news: If you've made it to this point in the book without having to employ a bookmark, there are at least a handful of colleges out there willing to accept you. But can you determine which school is best suited to your Overachieving Underperformer's ways?

The last thing you want is to find yourself stuck in a school that will demand more than you're willing to get others to help you put out. It's one thing to aim for a B when you could earn a better grade by actually studying. It's another to aim for a B because it's the best you can muster. Thus, you'll want to ensure that the majority of the other students at your college or university are at or below your intelligence level.

That being said, you can't simply enroll in a school where basic handwriting is a major. After all, if you're the only student who can put on your pants without bruising yourself, who will you copy your notes from? And, though you might graduate with honors, it's doubtful that you'll impress too many people with a degree in croquet.

Don't get stuck in a crowd you can't keep up with.

But you're not going to win any points by picking on those less fortunate than you.

So, without actually attending a semester at each of these types of schools, how can you tell which one is right for you? Perhaps the best method is to read the faces of those around you. Tell your teachers which schools you're planning on attending. If at the mention of a particular school, they raise an eyebrow in disbelief and say something doubtful like, "Um . . . you think that's a wise choice?" you should consider

Find a school where you're smarter than most, but where you can still find someone to edit your papers for you.

crossing that school off your list. If, conversely, they spit out their coffee and, amid paroxysms of laughter, congratulate you on the terribly funny joke, you'll know for certain that you are either way too dumb or way too intelligent to attend that school. As a rule, the less interest they display in your choice of school, the more you should be interested in it.

Chapter 2

AIM LOW, SHOOT LOW:
MINIMIZING YOUR GRADE EXPECTATIONS

Of the many myths about higher education, perhaps the most insidious is that your grades matter. Your parents convince you of this because they want to get the most for the money they're investing. Your professors impress this illusion upon you so as to justify their own existence. In truth, the marks you'll earn during your college years are of as much consequence as that embarrassing haircut you had when you were fifteen. Getting beyond this fallacy is paramount to the enjoyment of your pre–real world life.

B Is for Passing: That's Good Enough for Me

As is the case with most things in life, the answer to your problems is not entirely cut and dry. The first snag: You still need to pass your classes. Thus, unless you desire to put down your books and pick up a push broom, you'll need to be peripherally aware of how well you're underperforming in your various classes. Also, many schools set two levels of passing grades—one for your general classes and a second, higher standard for classes required for your major. So when consulting with your faculty adviser(s), be sure to discreetly inquire about any such distinctions.

Before entering into any field of study, talk to your adviser about what grades you'll need to pass.

Depending on your post-college aspirations, there might be some considerations for doing slightly better than the minimum. There are companies in this world that recruit new hires under the misguided belief that good grades translate into good employees. Not only will they ask you about your grades at the job interview, but they'll also actually have the temerity to demand a transcript. So unless you plan to master the fine art of document forgery, you'll want to have a transcript that's not going to make the interviewer collapse in a fit of laughter. This is why God created the B—low enough to be attainable by attending the occasional class, high enough to get you a job or (with some glowing faculty recommenda-

tions—see Chapter 26) into a lower-tier graduate program. Also, if your desired goal is to score a B, imagine the joy you'll give your parents (see Chapter 20) on the rare occasion when you manage to talk your way into something higher!

Impress your parents by doing slightly better than their diminished expectations.

Chapter 3

BE TRUANT TO YOUR SCHOOL:
WHY SHOWING UP LATE TO CLASS IS NOT NECESSARILY THE END OF YOUR COLLEGE CAREER

Let's take a second to shatter an underlying myth about the college classroom—the notion that you must arrive on time for every class. There's the age-old idea that if you are tardy, you must slip into the back row, hoping to go unnoticed. In fact, not only can you show up to some classes well into the lecture, but, with a bit of the old Overachieving Underperformer's magic, you can turn your lateness to your advantage.

① To Be or Not to Be in Class: Deciding Which Classes You Can Show Up Late for and Which Ones Are Better Left Unattended

As they represent two separate skill sets, the distinction needs to be made here between being tardy and being absent. You arrive late to class because you accidentally overslept, or because you stopped to talk to that cute pre-med student you ran into on the way to class. You skip class because you'd rather die than get out of bed, or because that cute pre-med student is in bed with you—and because there are certain classes that it would be in your best interest to miss entirely rather than arrive late.

Classes given in large halls with hundreds of faceless students' and lectures in the dark accompanied by interminable slide shows are easily invaded once they've begun. In fact, it would often be a *challenge* to be noticed arriving late to any of these classes. On the opposite end of the spectrum are the more intimate classes in which the professor takes attendance and makes an aggravating attempt to know his students' faces and names. These classes make things much more difficult for the Overachieving Underperformer.

Within the first week you should be able to suss out a particular professor's view on tardiness. If attendance is taken at the beginning of each lecture and if attendance is part of your final grade, you should at least make an effort to show up at some point to guarantee that you get your check mark for the day. If a professor takes attendance but does not calculate it into your final grade, you're free to skip if you so desire. But it's better to avoid than annoy those professors who—whether they take attendance or not—will mercilessly ride late-arriving students by quizzing them on the material they've missed. Instead, enjoy your freedom for the hour and go people watching at the student union. You'll be able to keep up with the course by scanning another student's notes later—and you'll often impress your professor with your ability to master the material through independent study.

② So You've Been Caught: How to Cope with the Shame of Tardiness

In the unfortunate event that you are noticed coming into class late, there's only a small need for concern. As mentioned above, there are those educators who will find their own amusement in grilling you in front of the entire class. If you unexpectedly find yourself the subject of such an interrogation, there are a couple of tactics to try.

Straightforward Humility—With a clear, unashamed voice, apologize to your professor and to your classmates for your lateness. Be sure not to come across as timid or meek, or the professor might attempt even further humiliation. You also want to be certain that the apology rings true, without even a hint of irony. This direct-yet-humble approach will tend to subdue your professor's chiding without causing him to feel that you've gotten the better of him. Also, the Overachievers in the class will appreciate your businesslike approach—which will make it much easier when you ask to photocopy their notes later.

Good-Natured Ribbing—A bolder gambit involves some playful banter. Despite the stereotype of the dry academic, most professors have a healthy sense of humor; they just tend not to show it whilst retreading the same lecture on the history of iron smelting that they've been giving for thirty-five years. This is your chance to let them demonstrate their wit. When taken to task for being late, tell your professor that you were on your deathbed and they were about to pull the plug when you said to yourself that there was no way you could die without making it to your economics seminar. Your professor may initially be taken aback at the gall of your statement but—should she have a sense of humor—will more than likely return with something along the lines of "That's the first right decision you've made this semester." If your statement elicits only a cold stare, quickly move to Straightforward Humility and put an emphasis on the Humility. Regardless of the reaction, take a few moments after class to approach your professor personally and feign a sincere apology. She'll be glad to see that you know your remark was uncalled for, and the two of you will have developed a personal bond that can be exploited later (see Chapter 26).

Chapter 4

A Seminar Missed Is a Nap Earned:
Your Guide to Missing Any Class

There are those irritating sticklers who will preach to you the virtue of perfect class attendance. These people have quite obviously never experienced the singular pleasure of sleeping until noon with the full knowledge that their peers are all the while busy scribbling notes in a drowsy haze. And in pragmatic terms, what benefit could you possibly derive from struggling through a lecture when the entirety of your thought is focused not on the pedantry at hand, but on the luxurious comfort of your bed? Napping is a necessity. Here are some helpful examples of what to say to miss that morning (or afternoon or evening) class without putting your college career to bed.

WARNING

Never, under any circumstances, tell your professor that you overslept. Remember that professors are people too . . . people with huge, fragile egos who would rather believe an outlandish lie than hear that you would prefer to sleep than listen to them speak.

① Tug of War

Example: "My poetry professor is going out of town for a book signing, and she rescheduled our class for this morning. She takes points off your grade if you miss a class."

Ideal Usage: For those professors who are convinced that all other faculty members are conspiring to have their tenures revoked. They will gleefully take any opportunity to cast blame upon a fellow professor, especially a professor with a well-regarded book. (See Chapter 16 for more on manipulating intra-faculty feuds.)

Frequency of Use: Can only be used once per semester per professor.

Believability: Depending on how much your professor loathes his fellow academics, there's nothing about this story that reeks of impossibility. It's much more believable for students in their first year of college, as it's more likely for a freshman than a senior to be bullied into missing a class to meet with a gallivanting professor.

Back Story: You'll need to have a professor with a book that merits a book signing. Unfortunately, they are not terribly common.

Pros: It's an excuse that might get you a mild scolding, but it will more than likely result in a simple "Next time this happens, tell me and I'll handle it."

Cons: Dangerous to use in a very small school where all faculty members know and converse with each other. Do not use if both professors are in the same academic department.

② Embarrassing Illness

Example: "Um... this is kind of embarrassing, but I was walking to class when I suddenly felt this feeling... down below."

Ideal Usage: For professors who are bookish, awkward, and withdrawn. These skittish folks will generally cut you off before you finish the sentence. At the other end of the spectrum, those professors who take pride in their candor and approachability will tend to get instantly wrapped up in a conversation about what could possibly be the source of your ills, and the fact that you blew off their class will completely leave their mind.

Frequency of Use: Employing this excuse more than twice a semester is not highly recommended, lest your professor become suspicious and demand a note from the medical center, or (worse) fear for your life and escort you to the hospital.

Believability: Everyone gets ill; more importantly, everyone acquires the occasional embarrassing malady. Any professor who can't sympathize with your feigned ordeal shouldn't be teaching.

Back Story: If your professor is the type who faints at the mention of bodily fluids, you shouldn't have to explain any further than pointing to the general area of your distress. For the biologically curious, you should be prepared to explain details that even you would not want to hear.

Pros: Fantastic catchall excuse. Could be used to get out of several classes in a single day without causing a problem.

Cons: There is always the risk that—after playing sick possum one day—you might actually find yourself ill soon thereafter. You don't want to engender suspicion of a past lie by being sick in reality.

OVERACHIEVING AT UNDERPERFORMING

If there is a bug making its way around campus and you're lucky enough to escape its viral touch, wait until it seems to have run its course before coming down with "that thing that was going around last week." Additionally, be sure to check the newspapers and medical Web sites for the latest information on what illnesses will likely be passing through your neighborhood. And it never hurts to have a friend who works in the college medical center and can keep you apprised of all disease-related developments.

Keep current on the latest disease-related developments so you'll know just when to skip class because you're "ill."

③ I'm with the Team

Example: "I'm the manager for the women's volleyball team, and we had to go out of town for a tournament."

Ideal Usage: For professors who are continually dropping sports references into the middle of their lectures. These people tend to value both academics and scholastic athletics, and often desire to be associated with their college's sports teams.

Frequency of Use: With the right professor, this can get you out of a snooze-inducing seminar up to three times a semester.

Believability: To the professor who will forever kick himself for not making the football team, your story is one he'll want to swallow. Just be sure that the particular team you work for is obscure . . . and that your excuse coincides with said team's season. Even the casual sports fan knows there is no college basketball in May.

Back Story: Be ready to answer how you got the gig, how much of your time the job requires, and is it really true about their . . . you-know-whats?

Pros: To the athletic-minded professor, you're a dream—someone involved with collegiate sports but without the attitude of entitlement.

Cons: You always run the risk that—no matter how obscure the sports team you select is—your professor might know everything about it, including the fact that you're not the manager. There is also the (very) slim chance that you might find yourself in a class with someone from the team you don't manage.

Chapter 5

BOOKS ARE FOR SUCKERS:
LIGHTENING THE LOAD IN YOUR BACKPACK

Four out of five chiropractors agree that the toting around of excess textbooks during one's college years is the main cause of back pain later in life.* Traveling from classroom to classroom across an expansive campus while laden with eight-hundred-page tomes (that only contain a dozen pages you'll need for the semester) can inflict severe damage to your shoulders and spine. Not to mention that these books cost more than a small house. Unfortunately, textbooks are an inevitability in the collegiate sphere. That is, unless you carry the Overachieving Underperformer's backpack—unburdened by those cumbersome texts and the undue stress they cause.

*Not an actual statistic, but chiropractors aren't actual doctors

Save Money, Make Money

Textbook publishers and the stores that sell their wares understand too well the notion of a captive audience. It's a merry-go-round process repeated every semester: The professor tells you which books to buy, and you trudge to the bookstore to pay whatever amount of flesh they demand. And at the end of the semester, after having turned no more than twenty pages in most of these books, you lug the essentially unused texts back to the store, where they take the books back and throw a handful of small change at you in return. The Overachieving Underperformer not only knows how to access these books for free, but also get paid while doing it.

The ultimate position of power at college isn't in the dean's office; it's behind the desk in the library.

All schools have libraries. (If your school doesn't have at least one library, you should check to make sure that you are actually attending a college and not just interrupting people at their place of work by raising your hand in the middle of meetings.) Beg and plead to whomever you can for a part-time job at the library. Why? Because most schools require that all professors put at least one copy of each required text on reserve in the library. This usually means that people can check out these books for only a very short period of time (typically two to four hours). However, since you're the one behind the desk, you've got control over whether or not a book is actually checked out. And if you work your way up to a manager position, you should also have free use of the copier in the office. Thus, even if you can't manage to keep a book from occasionally falling into other people's hands, you can just make no-charge copies of the few, significantly less heavy pages that you'll need.

> **WARNING**
>
> **If your school has several libraries, be sure to seek employment at the one where you'll find most of the books in your specific area of study. The law library does no good to an archaeology student.**

Even better than a job at the library is one at the source itself—the bookstore. Because there are always multiple copies of every book, you'll never have to worry about a fellow OU employee fake checking out the book from under your nose; just go snag another copy (preferably a used one, so as not to risk damaging a new book) off the shelf and read while you're working. Put it back when you're done. Furthermore, the bookstore should cover all subjects taught at your college, so there's no need to fret that you won't be able to find that book for that class you're taking out of your major (see Chapter 10). It's like having your own limitless reading room and getting paid for it!

OVERACHIEVING AT UNDERPERFORMING

As previously stated, there is the humiliating end-of-semester ritual whereby students return to the bookstore in an attempt to sell back the books purchased a few months earlier only to be told that what was so recently worth a nice meal for four is now worth the equivalent of a licorice whip. Desperate for anything resembling cash, students hang their heads and accept the pittance offered them. But what if someone offered them something just to the better side of stingy?

If you know what classes you'll be taking the next semester, find out where and when that class is being offered currently. Toward the end of the term, wait outside the room for the students to be dismissed, and when they emerge, make an announcement that you'll buy back someone's books for twice the insulting amount the bookstore is offering. At least one of them will take you up on your proposal. If you're lucky, you'll find yourself in a bidding war and only end up paying a few pennies above bookstore rate.

THE OVERACHIEVING UNDERPERFORMER'S
SEATING CHART

The worlds of real estate and academia seemingly have nothing in common. One deals with the buying, selling, and leasing of property; the other deals with the molding, shaping, and manipulation of the intellect. However, when dealing with where you should sit during class, the two subjects agree that three things matter: location, location, and location. Different classroom types pose different issues when it comes to seating, so here are a few guides to help you find that perfect seat with a view.

The Lecture Hall

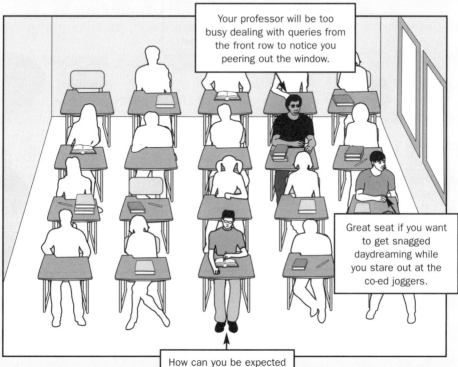

Chapter 6

BEING SEEN BUT NOT HEARD:
MAKING YOUR PRESENCE KNOWN WITHOUT EVER GETTING CALLED ON

So far, the Overachieving Underperformer's syllabus has guided you through the ins and outs of slipping into class late and staying out of class entirely. However, a grim inevitability exists—you will be required to attend at least a handful of classes. Even more dire is the possibility that simply because you're seated in the classroom, your professor might dare to engage you in the topic being taught. That prospect alone is enough to send weaker elements running for cover. But before you consider applying for an entry-level position at the car wash back home, be safe in the knowledge that all hope is not lost.

① Ask a Stupid Question...

It's highly likely that your class grade is based on a combination of in-class exams and at-home assignments. Thus, your behavior in the classroom often has little to no effect on your end-of-semester mark. That being said, you still don't want to be singled out when the professor asks questions of the students. Sure, you could hope that hiding in the back and not raising your hand will allow you to go undetected, but what about that day when your professor decides it's time to pick on the shy students? Not only do you prove yourself to be afraid of classroom participation, but you also risk being called out as a dunce. No, the easiest way to avoid being asked questions is to ask them yourself.

Be proactive. Don't let anyone tell you there are no such things as stupid questions. There most certainly are, and you should be the one asking them. But be careful. You'll want to select questions that—while a nuisance to your professor—don't make you out to be a complete fool. For instance, when your economics professor is lecturing on Milton Friedman, interrupt her and inquire about the spelling of Mr. Friedman's name, and then after she's finished spelling it out for you, repeat it back for clarification. Note: You don't want to make the mistake of asking her how to spell "Adam Smith," lest she deem you a moron and summarily toss you out of class.

In general, whenever your professor mentions a name, you're on safe ground asking for biographical information. "Did Abe Lincoln have any children?" "Where did Fitzgerald go to school?" Once again, be sure not to inquire about anything so obvious as "Didn't John F. Kennedy Jr.'s dad do something important?"

And because professors are really in love only with the sound of their own voices, when it comes time to ask students a question, the last voice they'll want to hear is the same one that just suggested further reading on the topic of petroleum refinement processes in 1970s Venezuela.

Pepper your professor with a barrage of questions, and she'll never want to call on you again.

OVERACHIEVING AT UNDERPERFORMING

Stupid questions aren't just good for keeping the professor from calling on you in class; they can be used for homework, too! When you ask some of your painfully obvious questions, you should actually make note of some of the answers for later. Thus, your paper on the Allied invasion of Normandy will contain sentences such as "When the Allied troops landed at Omaha Beach (which is in France and not Nebraska) on Wednesday, December 6, 1944, it was a major turning point in World War II (so named because the first

World War had occurred earlier in the century)." True, it's not a great, or even an adequately written, sentence, but all of the information is correct (and you're about twenty-five words closer to the one thousand required by your professor). Most important, you'll be showing her that you're not wasting her time in class with those inane inquiries; you really do need to know this stuff. She'll throw in a few bonus points for the extra effort and at least one pity point for good measure. And in a world where one point can mean the difference between another term of college fun or a lifetime of working the coal mine with Uncle Ted, you take what you can get.

② Getting into It

Barring some sort of random selection process, professors tend to call on two types of students: those with raised hands, begging to be called on, and those whose body language indicates a complete lack of interest in the subject matter. Keeping that in mind, you'll want to find a way to convince your professor that you are intrigued by what she's saying but you'd rather leave the question answering to the showboats in the front row.

There is a breed of Overachievers that rarely takes notes, because they are too intent on entering into a dialogue with the professor and showing how much they already know on the topic. Conversely, the Underperformers never take notes, because they don't care if they pass or not. What you've got to do is beat them both at their own games.

While your professor is speaking, you should be pretending to take a continuous stream of notes. Make sure to look up periodically from your scribbling and make eye contact with the professor. Biting your lip in the name of feigned intensity couldn't hurt. When a student answers a question, pause momentarily and look in the direction of that student before going right back to your non-notes. In reality you're jotting down a to-do list for the party you're planning, but the professor sees a student who is neither a show-off nor a slacker, but rather someone who's interested in the material and believes that it's best learned by quietly listening to the more experienced professor.

Pretend to be interested in what's being taught and your professor won't single you out to be called on.

Chapter 7

OF BASEBALL CAPS AND SLIDE SHOWS:
NAPPING THROUGH LECTURES WITH IMPUNITY

Part of the OU code is planning for the unexpected. Suppose your morning is going perfectly and you were able to slip undetected into your class twenty minutes late; you even got a little bite to eat on the walk over. And then the professor suddenly dims the lights and the room fills with the familiar hum of the slide projector. The desire to close one's eyes is inescapable. Why fight it? With the right napping game plan, there's no reason to.

① Staying Out of the Limelight

Next to cheating, the last thing you want to get caught doing in a college classroom is sleeping. Thus it's in your best interest to make yourself as inconspicuous as possible. In that regard there are two options.

First and most practical is to simply make an exit once the lights are dimmed. After all, the odds of your remaining conscious during the lecture are slim, so you might as well spend the time sleeping outside under a tree or on a hallway couch.

WARNING

If you plan to sleep anywhere in the vicinity of the classroom you're leaving, be sure to set an alarm on your cell phone so you wake up before class lets out. Few moments are more humiliating than groggily coming to as your entire class and professor stand around glaring at your obvious laziness.

But perhaps you can't exit the room without walking directly by the professor. Or maybe you know that girl you're avoiding is lingering in the hallway outside. When escape from the classroom is impossible, a second option is to stay in the room and do your sleeping there. Since the slide projector will illuminate some areas of the room more than other parts, you'd be best served to find a seat in the darkest section. If you're in a lecture hall where the projector is located in a booth at the rear of the room, the ideal seat is directly below or next to the projector's lens. Because the lens is the brightest spot in the room and no one can look at it straight on, you've managed to situate yourself in a position where you can doze away without the professor even looking in your direction.

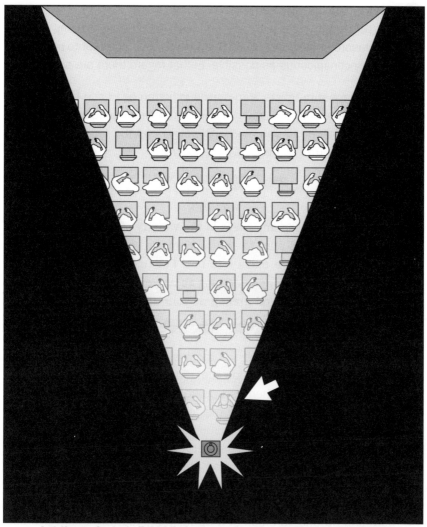

Let the projector's light blind your professor and allow you to sleep.

② Napping Essentials

If you're going to nod off in the classroom, there are a handful of things you'll need to be aware of before you shut your eyes.

- Sit next to an Overachiever. It's possible that you might annoy her slightly, but she generally won't rat you out or wake you up so long as you don't disturb her. And the instant you emit a sound even vaguely snore-like, she'll pinch you awake faster than you can say "grade grubber." She might abide your little nap, but there's no way she's going to let you snore and attract any negative attention from the professor.

- Be aware if you have a tendency to talk in your sleep. Ask a girl-friend/boyfriend, roommate, or close friend to observe you while you sleep one night to make sure you're not prone to unconscious displays of verbosity. You don't want to interrupt the entire class by blurting out, "The Canadians have the keys, and they won't give them back until Bob answers his phone on Monday!" There are some things even the best OU can't talk his way out of.

- Even if you're on the team, never wear a baseball cap. The visor only accentuates any head nodding that might occur as part of the sleep process. Whether it's pointing straight up because your head is falling back or straight into your lap because your chin is resting on your chest, your baseball cap might as well be a huge red flag sticking out of your neck.

  If you absolutely must wear a baseball cap, wear it backward, so as to minimize the chances of sending up your own red flag. Also, if you have a tendency to let your head fall backward while sleeping, the visor might assist in keeping your head upright.

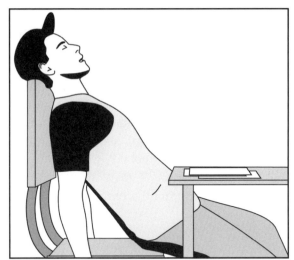

"Hey, look at me sleeping!"

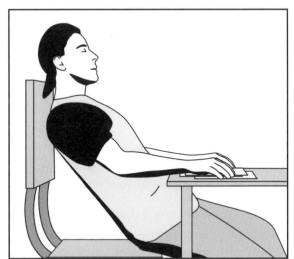

"I'm learning with my eyes closed."

- Learn to sleep sitting up. Do not use the top of your desk as a sleeping surface. Even if your professor can't see your closed eyes or hear your quiet snoring, it takes only a momentary glimpse of you slumped over the desk to know that you're sleeping. There is no possible way for you to write notes when your face occupies the entirety of your writing surface. People also tend to drool less when sleeping upright.

- Invest in those mini-strips that are placed on the bridge of your nose to relieve nasal congestion—they also help to relieve the noise pollution caused by your snoring.

Looking Smart, Playing the Part:
Dressing Like an Academic Without Really Being One

The phrase "model student" is often bandied about to describe the typical overachieving young academic. As such, it implies that said student is one whose study ethic and classroom demeanor should be used as an example for others to follow. However, in the malleable grammar of the Overachieving Underperformer, a model student is one who improves his grades by modeling his dress and behavior after his professors'.

There was once a time when attiring oneself in a professor's garb was a somewhat simple matter of picking out the correct tweed sport coat and brown loafers. However, the species has evolved into a veritable cornucopia of typologies. Herewith are some examples of the more prevalent and timeless of fashions you'll find roaming the halls.

① The Dinosaur

A throwback to a time when the only women on campus were professors' wives. It's a look that shouts (in a politely demanding voice), "I'm here to learn, not to drink to excess and vomit into my roommate's sock drawer." Your professor will notice you and be glad to see that he's not alone in his fight against those who can't be bothered to take their dress (and, by extension, their classwork) seriously. And while you may initially find your fellow students casting a leery glance in your direction, all that's required is for you to tell the ones whom you want to befriend that you're being ironic.

Accessory Note: An antique pocket watch adds just a dash of old-timey earnestness that says to your professor, "I'm not one of these overgrown brats."

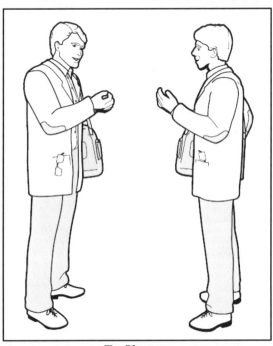

The Dinosaur

② The Eccentric

These professors are either desperate for attention or color-blind, sometimes both. The look is unisex, so you're in a good position

The Eccentric

whatever the gender of your professor. And while wearing a scarf all year round might be a minor annoyance, any discomfort will be allayed by the fact that your professor finds you agreeable enough to grant you an extension on your paper. Not to mention all the dates you'll get with the art students.

Accessory Note: A sketchbook or (preferably) a large portfolio is the right item to tote around for that added air of mystery.

③ The Explorer

Here's the professor who regales students with tales from his latest safari trek or archaeological dig. He's serious, but he's not about to put on a tie. Despite his almost casual appearance, he doesn't abide students who don't share his passion. Thus, when he hears someone snoring in the back of the classroom while he shows slides of the Serengeti, he certainly won't assume it's you in all your full-khaki glory, complete with hiking boots.

Accessory Note: It couldn't hurt to show up to class with an impressive-looking camera slung around your shoulder. Bonus points if you can find a matching vest in which to stow your film.

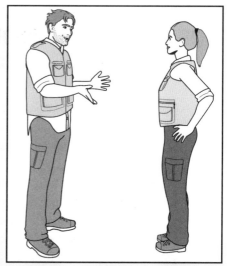

The Explorer

OVERACHIEVING AT UNDERPERFORMING

Most professors forever harbor an unflagging belief that the university from which they received their education is the end-all, be-all of academic life. So it's in your best interest to find out where they originally cut their scholarly teeth. Such information is rarely difficult to come by, as it's usually on display on their office walls. Once you've done the detective work, it's time to stock up on as much paraphernalia (sweatshirts, hats, pins, coffee mugs) as possible. Make an effort to be seen wearing or holding these items by your professor (the more obvious the better). If you've done everything correctly, he'll inquire as to why you're wearing a hat from another university. Explain that—while you really love the education that you're getting now—you hope to attend that school for graduate study. This may or may not lead to your professor mentioning that he is an alumnus of the school in question. Regardless, he now has it in his head that the two of you are like-minded.

SECTION II
Course Selection

Now that you understand all the basics of when and how to miss your classes, it's high time you learn something about picking these courses. Ask yourself a few questions: Do you mind waking up before lunchtime? Do you like being challenged academically? Do you enjoy being tested weekly? If you're reading this book, your answer for all of these questions is more than likely a resounding "no." These next chapters will help you to both sidestep some nasty curricular traps and free yourself should you find yourself caught in one.

Chapter 8

THE FINALS COUNTDOWN:
JUDGING A CLASS BY ITS COVER

For the incoming college student, the process of choosing which classes to take is often like shooting in the dark. All first-year students generally have at least one or two required courses, but what about the rest of your week? Unless you have friends with a semester or two under their belts who can advise which courses are easily aced and which professors should be avoided at all cost, you've very little to go on except the vague description listed in the school's catalog. It's a daunting situation, to say the least. But if you study up on your classes before they begin, you won't have to study much at all once the semester's started.

Before the session begins, most professors will make detailed course descriptions available either online or through their department offices. Often these not only will give an outline for the subjects to be touched upon during the class, but also will describe how students' grades are determined, i.e., what percentage of your mark comes from papers versus exams, how many exams will be given, and if class participation and attendance are included in the equation. There are almost infinite permutations of these factors, and it would be impossible to run through them all. However, there are a few general configurations that bear examination.

① All or Nothing

This is a class where a final exam is the only deciding factor in your grade. To some students this is the Holy Grail, allowing them to get credit for showing up to class once. For them, it's a matter of scanning the textbooks and attending a few study sessions with people who actually attended the class. However, you should be forewarned that success in a class like this depends on your ability to memorize a lot of information in an extremely short period of time. Also, these classes tend to bring out the slacker in most everyone; chances are, the "study session" you're banking on milking for answers is stocked with others who opted not to attend lectures. Taking an All or Nothing class could be a dangerous prospect, but the risk might pay off in the form of extra hours flirting with that cutie at the coffee shop.

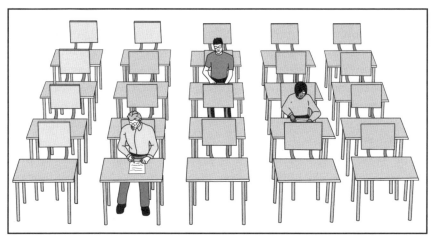

Classes in which your entire grade is determined by the final tend to be empty all semester...

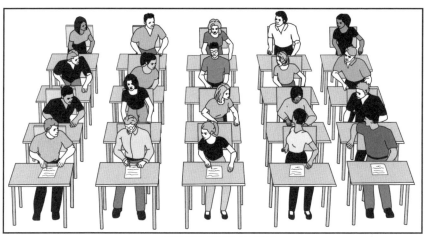

...until the study session.

TIP It always helps to go into a class knowing in advance that you'll have someone from whom to glom dependable notes. An Overachieving roommate or sorority sister—preferably one who's not judgmental—is ideal. This is true for all breeds of college course but especially for the All or Nothing class, where you might not even dare enter without such a friend.

② Half and Half

Here you have a professor who wants to make sure that at least a third of the class shows up for every lecture. She does this by splitting students' grades between a paper assigned halfway through the semester and a final exam at the end. And while, yes, this does require that you occasionally make an appearance in the classroom, it also presents an opportunity for you to employ the Horrifying First Draft (described in detail in Chapter 13). Also, since you'll have some sort of idea where you stand grade-wise after the paper, you can plan how much or how little you need to study for the rest of the semester.

TIP If it's not noted on the course description, try to find out whether exams in the class are multiple choice or essay by questioning either former students or the professor herself. Multiple choice is preferred, but if you get stuck facing an essay exam, be sure not to leave anything blank. Half of an incorrect answer will generally earn you more points than no answer at all.

③ The Weekly Woe

When a professor is so insecure that he feels required to quiz his students on a weekly basis, you've got a slight problem. And since these once-a-week annoyances usually deal solely with topics discussed in that week's class and may cover issues beyond what's covered in the texts, you've got to either get very good at borrowing an Overachiever's notes (more on that in Chapter 18) or show up to class. The only real upside to a class like this is that it gives an Overachieving Underperformer the chance to hone his Room for Improvement technique (as explained in Chapter 11). Otherwise, try to minimize the number of these classes that fall into your schedule.

④ Welcome to Your Nightmare

At least once in your college experience you will find yourself stranded in a class where there are not only midterm and final exams but also periodic in-class quizzes and papers to write at home . . . and attendance is taken every session. And sometimes attendance isn't just taken—you're graded every day on your level of participation. Classes like this are why most colleges allow you to drop courses during the first month of the term. If the class is required for your major, change your major. At the very least, you won't have an F on your transcript, and this midway altering of your academic arc might help you put that Six-Year Plan (see Chapter 22) into action.

Chapter 9

What Does "a.m." Stand For?:
Why Morning Classes Might Not Be So Horrible

Whether it's a shrill chirping, a steady buzz, a piercing bell, or just a local radio station, there are few sounds more unpleasant to a student than the sound of his alarm going off in the morning. Most students instinctively shy away from any class that begins before the morning hours reach double digits, and not without good reason. Of course, there are some students who actually *like* waking up while the moon is still out, and morning classes are fine for them. But whatever your disposition toward the early hours of the school day, you should consider the following benefits of taking a morning class.

① Never to Bed, Early to Rise

Just about every college student has the occasional mid-week late night out with friends. Many students have these nights on a regular basis. This is precisely why those same students look with disdain on the idea of attending an early class. Common sense dictates that you'd be better served by skipping that morning lecture and getting some extra sleep so you don't ruin the rest of your day. On this count, common sense isn't being very sensible.

Consider the following: Which looks worse—your appearance after no sleep or your appearance after two hours of sleep? Chances are, they don't look very different. Thus, you've nothing to worry about in terms of looking tired or sleepy in front of your professor. So when you get home at four in the morning, it's best to put on a pot of coffee and watch some TV until it's breakfast time. Grab yourself some juice and a muffin. You'll most likely be just fine by the time class rolls around. Remember—you only need to remain lucid for ninety minutes or so. And if your lack of sleep brings on a bit of giddy dementia, it will only serve to make that lecture on the Polynesian candlestick industry more interesting.

You're going to look like this at 8 a.m. whether or not you've actually slept.

OVERACHIEVING AT UNDERPERFORMING

As discussed above, unless you're the rare Overachieving Underperformer who rises before the sun every day, you're going to look at least mildly disheveled at your morning class. Take advantage of this fact. After class, approach your professor and apologize for looking like a loaf of week-old bread. Explain that you had gone out of town to see to a family matter but took the overnight train back to campus so you could make it to class on time. Be sure to imply that this specific class was the one that caused you to return early. You might even want to say you haven't even had time to shower or change your clothes. Your professor will be impressed with and flattered by your dedication to her class.

② Siesta Fiesta

Another thing to think about when trying to decide whether or not to take a morning class is how it can actually help you miss some of your classes later in the day. Unless you're one of the early rising folks mentioned earlier, you will inevitably find yourself exhausted by lunchtime if you go to your morning class. Occasionally you'll be struggling just to make it to an afternoon class. Well, go ahead and take that siesta if you need it! If your professor makes an inquiry about your absence, be prepared with a solid excuse (see Chapter 4 for examples). Unlike professors who teach morning classes and assume that an empty seat equals a sleeping student, professors who teach classes in the afternoon are more likely to believe your alibi—after all, you couldn't have been asleep all day if you made it to your morning classes. If they don't believe you, they can just go and ask the professors whose classes you didn't sleep through!

③ Professor Appreciation

Professors know that students are loath to attend classes before noon. After enough years of lecturing to half-empty auditoriums and foggy-eyed students, most tend to accept this behavior as a given. However, just because your professor has become inured to his students' choosing rest over research doesn't mean that he won't appreciate the rare student who doesn't just drag her semicomatose body to class, but who actually appears to *want to be* in his class, regardless of the time.

Show your professor you want to be in his a.m. class, and he'll cut you some slack.

Thus, whether you're a natural early riser or you've just managed to wake up that morning, it behooves you to set yourself apart from the other a.m. zombies who limp into the room. Bring an extra cup of coffee to class and offer it to your professor (be prepared with cream and sugar if necessary). When you have a chance, say something to the professor along the lines of "It's a real shame that your class is so early in the morning. These people who won't take morning classes are really missing out on something important." Professors, who automatically assume their students do not want to be there, are always delighted to hear anything that sounds remotely like genuine admiration (for another example of this, see Chapter 16). Also, a student who shows up ten minutes late but who by all appearances wants to be there is often cut more slack than the dozing few who made it to class on time.

Slaying the "Dragon Lady":
Taking Classes That Others Avoid

In every college, in just about every department, there exists at least one universally dreaded professor. The "Dragon Lady," the "Slave Driver," the "Hard-ass"—all terms for essentially the same thing—a professor who demands excellence from her students. In general, you'd be wise to cut these professors a wide berth. But every once in a great while, it might serve you well to venture into the Dragon Lady's lair.

① Falling on Your Own Sword
One trait common to these whip-cracking professors is that they despise smugness in anyone except themselves. Every semester they are faced with at least a dozen foolish Overachievers who not only sincerely believe that they're going to do well in the class, but also make a point of behaving as if they've already earned that A. When a question is asked, they're the first with their hands in the air, desperately trying to impress. These are also the first students the Dragon Lady devours wholesale just to make examples of them.

So try a little humility. After a week or so, approach the Dragon Lady after class or during her office hours. Tell her that you find her class enthralling but that you feel you could be doing a little better. Mention that you're a little intimidated by the hand-raisers. Whether she says so or not, she'll agree with you. It's not going to change how she teaches the class or how often the Overachievers try to hog her attention, but she'll remember who you are. And when it comes time to grade your paper, she'll be more impressed by your earnest but obtuse writing than she will be with the validation-seeking tracts of the others.

② Battle Scars

Another truism with regard to Dragon Lady types is that—in addition to the handful of students who are taking the class for a gold star on their transcripts—there are many students who will not pass her class. Furthermore, many professors of this ilk are renowned for their sternness, not just among the faculty of your college, but in many other colleges as well. Thus, if you can somehow manage simply to earn a passing grade, you'll merit a badge of honor among those in the know. When you apply to graduate school, what ostensibly appears to be a black eye on your transcript will be seen as merely a bruise by people who understand the Dragon Lady's reputation.

③ If at First You Don't Succeed, Try Try an Easier Class

If, sadly, you are one of the many who do not manage to pass the Dragon Lady's class, don't fret; life will go on (in fact you may have just bought yourself another semester of avoiding the real world!), and it is certainly not the end of your college education. Explain to your parents the frequency with which the Dragon Lady fails her students. You might be able to convince them that—since you won't have the credits from the failed class—you need to take a course during the summer session (see Chapter 23) to maintain your goal of graduating in less than a decade. At the very least, when you take an easier course the next semester, your parents will be elated at your beautiful B.

Chapter 10

STUDYING OUTSIDE THE BOX:
TAKING CLASSES IN OTHER FIELDS OF STUDY

It may first appear that the most direct approach to making your way through college with minimal work and maximum results is picking a course of study that you're vaguely familiar with and sticking to it as firmly as possible. However, there is much to be said for stepping beyond the bounds of your particular field of semi-study.

① The Outsider Factor

Many professors and students enjoy having the opportunity to introduce someone new to their specialized academic areas; the more obscure the subject matter, the greater the desire to convince the outsider of its merits. Taking advantage of this desire, stepping into a classroom where the pupils are studying a topic you don't even know how to pronounce can not only allow you to maintain your mediocre grade point average but also be a boon to your transcript.

Explain to the professor that, though it's something well outside of your normal interests, you've heard such amazing things about her class from another student that you'd kick yourself if you didn't enroll. You've instantly positioned yourself as an eager neophyte, someone willing to expand his or her understanding of the world. More importantly, your professor will invariably grade you on a curve, judging your work by a more flexible (read: lower) standard than the other students. When you turn in an assignment and your professor finds a majority of your answers misguided or entirely incorrect, she'll assume that it's simply due to your lack of background on the topic and not because you have yet to read any of the required chapters. What would have been a D for anyone else in the class is a passable C for you.

OVERACHIEVING AT UNDERPERFORMING

And you can improve your marks further: Approach your professor after class or during her office hours and ask to review the assignment. In the course of your discussion, you need to appear fascinated by what she tells you, as if she is miraculously clearing away all the confusion from your mind. After each point she makes, simply restate what she's told you and take some notes. Beg and plead for an opportunity to do the assignment over. Tell her that it's not about the grade; you just want to make sure you're getting as much out of the class as you can. Then, after turning in a second pass at the assignment (which she's essentially done for you), sit back and watch as that C blossoms into a solid B!

② **Expanding Your Social Circle**

Breaking new ground academically also means breaking new ground socially. If you're intruding on a class filled with people who have all been taking classes together for several terms, many of your fellow students will leap at the chance to meet someone outside of their academic sphere. (The ultimate example of this can be found in Chapter 20.)

While it's always nice to make new friends, it's even better to make new study partners. By taking one class outside of your major, you've managed to surround yourself with people with entirely new skills sets. Take a class on German literature (taught using English translations, of course), and there's guaranteed to be someone there who is fluent

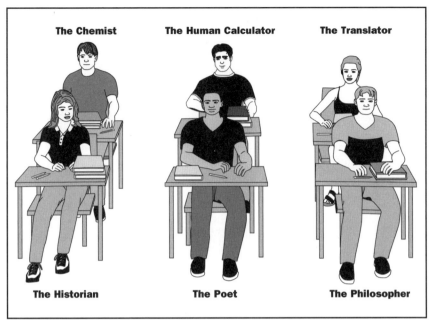

The Chemist **The Human Calculator** **The Translator**

The Historian **The Poet** **The Philosopher**

Take classes outside of your major and make study buddies in other fields.

in German, which you need to fill your language requirement. Take a class in the astronomy department, and there will always be someone in the class whose grasp of numbers is so great that he hasn't had to use a calculator since kindergarten. Depending on your particular academic weaknesses, there are history buffs, book lovers, walking dictionaries, and many other helpful study buddies waiting for you in strange classrooms all over campus.

SECTION III
Classwork

Unfortunately, there is only so much sleeping, drinking, eating, and socializing a young academic can handle. You'll eventually have to attend a class, which means that you will eventually have to do work. Lucky for you, the Overachieving Underperformer has several methods for minimizing both the quantity and quality of the work you'll need to do. These time-honored manipulations will—almost magically—transform your mediocre C drudgery into a respectable B endeavor.

Chapter 11

ROOM FOR IMPROVEMENT: WHY PLAYING DUMB FOR THE FIRST HALF OF A SEMESTER TRANSLATES INTO A HIGHER GRADE IN THE END

Every college student who has ever had an academically disappointing semester has begun the next term by vowing to hit the ground running from day one. They fill their head with silly mantras: "Work smarter AND harder!" "Focus focus focus!" "No more beer at breakfast!" This is, of course, one of the more common (and potentially damaging) mistakes that you can make. Not only is it nearly impossible to maintain a high level of intensity for the requisite four or five months, but the inevitable downfall (usually occurring somewhere around week two) tends to lead down the path to depression when, once again, you haven't been able to live up to your New Semester's resolutions. So why sprint headlong toward failure when you can just as easily take baby steps toward a passing grade?

① Mapping Your Lack of Progress

Generally speaking, there are thirteen to fifteen weeks in a semester. Consider yourself well advised to utilize them all. The goal here is to demonstrate to your professor that her lectures and lessons are working their way into your seemingly thick head. The alternative is the last-minute cram: There is a chance that she might be impressed with a miracle end-of-term turnaround, but more often than not your professor will assume that you could've done better all semester and she'll grade you as sternly as (if not more so than) those who've actually been studying. Better to stretch it out.

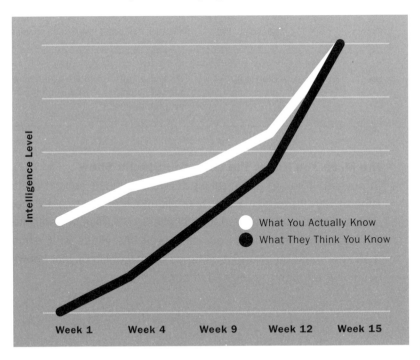

② Different Strokes for Different Curricula

Each type of class poses a particular set of issues for the Overachieving Underperformer. Here is a handy chart to show how you'll need to progress up the ladder from "idiot" to "dullard" to "adequate."

Type of Class	Starting Point	Mid-Term	End Objective
Weekly quizzes	Get your name wrong	Don't leave any questions blank	Don't answer any questions with "I dunno"
Essays	Misspell "the"	Misspell "inability"	Misspell "priapism"
Lab	Start a fire while dissecting a frog	Dissect a frog without cutting your lab partner	Start a fire using a Bunsen burner

③ The More You Know, the Less You Should Show

Of course, if you're stuck taking a course whose subject matter is alien to you, it probably won't take too much acting to convince your professor that you've moved from clueless to sufficiently enlightened. But for those times that you can enroll in a class with a familiar topic, you must be aware at all times of how much of your knowledge is shining through the feigned idiocy.

For example, suppose you're a real art history nut. Not only do you not want to get caught correcting your professor's pronunciation of Wassily Kandinsky's name in the early weeks of the semester, but you should also appear to be so daft as to confuse Kandinsky with Dick Kryhoski, who hit sixteen homeruns for St. Louis in 1951. Furthermore, the more ridiculous your question or statement, the more you need to make sure that it's heard by everyone.

As the semester improves and your responses in class become less and less addle-brained, your professor will begin to give you full credit for answers that would have earned other students nothing but scorn. The professor will feel validated that even the densest of students could learn from his sagacious teachings, and you'll walk out at the end of the semester with a much better grade than you deserve.

Chapter 12

"PROTÉGÉ" IS NOT A DIRTY WORD:
BECOMING YOUR PROFESSOR'S PET PROJECT

Many professors take a less-than-loving view toward most of their students. Years of being both besieged by grade-grubbing Overachievers and utterly ignored by Underperformers tend to rob academic types of their once-idealistic attitudes. Thus, when the rare student who shows initiative comes around seeking his professor's guidance, it's enough to blind the professor to the fact that said student hasn't been to class since the first week of the semester.

Office Hours = Quality Time

Most colleges require all professors to be available for a certain number of hours, office hours, each week for their students to come by and discuss their class work. It also affords you the perfect opportunity to insinuate yourself into the professor's world.

Early in the term approach your professor during her appointed hours. Explain to her that you think you might have overloaded your course schedule for the semester. You could drop one of your classes to make things easier, but her seminar is the only class on your schedule that's not required for your major, which means it would have to be her class that gets the axe. Offer up the following suggestion: To make sure that you maintain your focus on her class, and that it gets the attention it deserves, would it be possible for you to come in for a few minutes (no longer than a half hour) every week or two so that she can review what's going on in class? Your professor will be impressed with your dedication, and agree to your proposition.

TIP Try out this technique on a professor whose only available hours don't interfere with your favorite soaps.

During this time spent with your professor, she will spell out for you everything that's been covered in class since your last meeting. She'll assume that it's all a matter of recapping the lectures, when really you're hearing most of this for the first time. Don't limit yourself to in-class issues. Ask her to explain the reading, and she'll gladly guide you through it (especially if it's something she wrote). Essentially, with a biweekly, thirty-minute meeting, you can all but eliminate the need to attend a twice-weekly, sixty-minute lecture or do any of the required reading.

**Getting your professor personally invested in your work
will get you out of having to do any reading.**

Chapter 13

Wow Them with Mediocrity:
Why It's to Your Advantage to Turn In a Horrifying First Draft

How often have you been told that the first impression you make on someone is the most important? That the more sour the taste left in someone's mouth after first meeting you, the deeper the pit you find yourself plunged into? It's a sentiment that's been repeated so often by so many that most deem it to be axiomatic. But the Overachieving Underperformer is not like most people. It's not fatal to get off on the wrong foot. In fact, it just might help you win the race.

Beating the (First) Draft: A Word Problem

Consider the following scenario: There are two students, A and B, in Professor D's ethics class. They are both assigned a paper on the same subject.

Student A is a classic Overachiever and begins researching the topic immediately upon receiving the assignment. He writes three drafts before he even considers showing it to Professor D. And when he finally turns it in, he presents it in pristine form, complete with a cover sheet (the preemptive apologia "rough draft" featured prominently).

Student B handwrites a first draft in chicken scratch, her information based solely on the notes she borrowed from Student A (see Chapter 18 for tips on this). Her first draft would more accurately be termed a rough outline. Of the few sentences written, her grammar is atrocious and her spelling is at about the level of a third grader who just emigrated from a country that uses a different alphabet.

Question: Who gets the better grade?

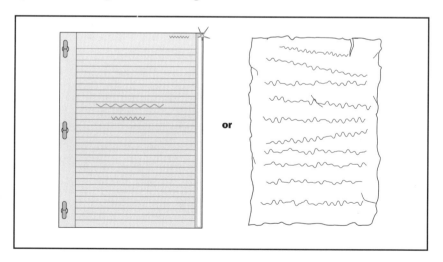

Answer: Believe it or not, Student B has the better chance of ending up with a high grade in this instance. At the very least, Student B will end up with a grade on her final paper that is much better than she deserves. To understand why this is, let's take a closer look at what happens after these two disparate first drafts are handed in.

Student A's first draft is impeccable. Well-researched, clearly and cleanly presented, it is everything a final paper should be. It's also a tremendous waste of the professor's time. When Student A's draft is handed over to Professor D, all that's really there to critique are some minor grammatical errors and a handful of typos. This paper isn't going to improve substantially between first and final drafts. In fact, there is the possibility that it might get worse as Student A compulsively tinkers with it.

Student B's first draft (for want of a better term) is worthy of the dustbin. Professor D's immediate reaction is shock and dismay. He'll want to schedule some office time with Student B, ostensibly to review her draft but mostly to make sure she doesn't suffer from severe brain damage. In this one-on-one session, Student B apologizes for the slipshod first draft—she was just attempting to get everything out of her head and onto paper as quickly as she could—and gushes about how happy she is to have this chance to work things out with Professor D. Once it's clear that B is not the complete idiot her original draft would make her out to be, the professor will begin to go over B's "outline" in a very clear and deliberate manner. B will, for one of the rare moments in her semester, take down what Professor D tells her. After thirty minutes to an hour of this discussion, the professor will have unwittingly written B's paper for her. All that's left for her to do is neatly type it up and put a cover sheet on it. In the space of one meeting, she's accomplished what took Student A two wasted weekends at the library.

The end result is that both Students A and B turn in comparable final products. But based solely on the phenomenal level of improvement demonstrated in B's paper, her work will represent a more stunning progression, thereby elevating her grade to a disproportionately high level. Student A, on the other hand, will get either the exact grade he would have received if he had simply turned in his first draft or—since it shows no real improvement—a slightly lesser one.

THE POWER OF BABBLE:
PUTTING COMPUTER GIBBERISH TO GOOD USE

In any student's life, there are times when a deadline looms but a few more hours of writing time are required to finish the assignment. Luckily, in the e-mail age the Overachieving Underperformer is not without a remedy.

If you've been up all night writing that paper (the one you've had all semester to work on) and you realize that the odds of finishing before your eleven o'clock class are about as good as the Expos winning the World Series, it's time to hitch a ride on the information superhighway. Save a copy of the paper you've been working on under a separate file name. Go into this file and begin rolling your head back and forth along the keyboard. It helps if you can manage to hold down the control and command keys so you get some of those keyboard oddities mixed in (Ô, Î, ©, Σ,Á, ∏). Then cut and paste this gibberish all over your paper. It helps if you can add about thirty pages of squiggles and nonsense at the end. You should now have something that looks like this:

> When analyzing the fiscal policies of the administration, one must remember to ß††¥ †˙ øπ®å†ˆ◊ÇØÂÂÅ˜∂ß WØÓˆØ˜Ï·º,™•¨º‡ ´Ç◊Ç´Ø˜Í ˘Ø ˘ÓØ±ˆÍ ‰¨˙Ò´ ØÏ ÇØÎ‰ʻÍ˙ ÏØÒÒØ„˘ Ø˜ÒÒÅå¬Σå¥ß ß†å†ø®∂∂çø†©ßß†¨˙∂†¥ †˙ øπ®å†ˆ◊´ ÇØÂÂÅ˜∂ß WØÓˆØ˜Ï·º,™•º‡ ´Ç◊Ç´Ø˜Í ˘Ø ˘ÓØ±ˆÍ ‰¨˙Ò´ ØÏ ÇØÎ‰ʻÍ˙ ÏØÒÒØ„˘ Ø˜ÒÒÅå¬Σå¥ß ß † å † ø ® ∂ ∂ ç ø † © ß ß ‰ Í ´ Ï Ø Ò Ò Ø „ ˘ Ø ˜ Ò Ò Å å ¬ Σ å ¥ ß ß†å†ø®∂∂çø†©ßß†¨¨∂†¥ †˙ øπ®å†ˆ◊´ ÇØÂÂÅ∂ßWØÓˆ™•¨º‡ ´Ç◊Ç´Ø˜Í ˘Ø ˘ÓÏ ÇØÎ‰ʻÍ˙ ÏØÒÒØ„˘ Ø˜ÒÒÅå¬Σå¥ß ß†å†ø®∂çø†©ß will only lead to confusion and chaos within the marketplace.

Compose an e-mail to your professor explaining that you are too ill to attend class but you wanted to make sure the paper was received on time. Then attach the garbled document. Chances are, your professor won't even try to open the attachment until after she gets around to reading and grading everyone's paper, by which point you would have already handed in the assignment you finished two days late. If she does open the file, she'll assume it was corrupted in the transfer. She might ask you to resend the paper, so do as she asks and resend that same nonsense file. As e-exasperation sets in, she'll cave in and just ask for you to bring the printed out assignment to her office when you're able to—hours, even days, after the true deadline.

Chapter 14

STUDIOUS BY ASSOCIATION:
HANGING AROUND BOOKWORMS TO IMPROVE YOUR GPA

When it comes to groups of people, we tend to assume that all mem-bers of a group possess the same general characteristics. This is the reason your mother never liked you playing with the dirty kids down the block when you were eight—because she knew that other people would begin to think of you as one of those dirty kids. And this is precisely why your mother was always trying to force you into play dates with the smart kid whose parents made him wear a tie to school.

In this chapter, you'll see that your mother was right.

**After a lecture join the group of Overachievers
who always linger to ask questions.**

Make sure to grab the empty seat at the study-buddy table in the cafeteria.

Just because people think you're reading doesn't mean you actually are.

OVERACHIEVING AT UNDERPERFORMING

While many college Overachievers are well-known by the students at their schools, it's usually because they're the ones who run all the student organizations and (non-fun) clubs on campus. However, as their desire to succeed is often fueled by a deeply ingrained yearning for validation and acceptance, they feel the need to be respected by *all* of their fellow students, even the slacking Underperformers. This is why you need to keep them apart from your beer-swilling, barely passing pals. Once heard, the siren song of the lazy life is difficult to resist, and that Overachiever who lends you his notes can all too quickly become an Underperformer asking to borrow yours. And even if the studious one doesn't fall from grace, by having your two worlds meet you're granting your slothful drinking buddies access to your private stock of Overachievers. How can you expect to ask your history Overachiever to edit your paper when his schedule is filled by all of your friends' assignments?

A solution, of course, exists: Figure out which of your Overachiever's many odd quirks your partying pals are most likely to find geeky or off-putting. Then introduce him to your friends, making certain that he demonstrates this peculiarity. When the dust clears, your indolent friends will mock you for acquainting yourself with such a nerd, while said nerd will not have liked the icy reception he received. Shrug your shoulders to both parties and say, "Oh well. Different strokes for different folks." Voila! Your two worlds are safely distanced, and you can mooch notes and homework without interference.

Chapter 15

MEALS ON TOOTHPICKS: WHY IT MAKES GOOD DIETARY SENSE TO ATTEND BORING FACULTY FUNCTIONS

For most university students, their time outside of class—whether playing or studying—should be professor free. Even students who don't mind their professors still choose not to spend their free hours with them. From a social standpoint, this is understandable—the gap in ages and interests, the discrepancy in generational references, the fact that most professors choose wine and cheese over malt liquor and pizza. But this is a very shortsighted outlook on things. Spending time with your professors can be a spiritually rewarding experience, allowing you to learn life lessons from the older generation while invigorating the somewhat stale life of an academic. Friends learn from each other. They also give extensions on overdue papers.

① Lectures and Lunches: The Horror . . . the Horror

Most professors enjoy nothing more than the dulcet tones of their own voices booming over a PA system to an appreciative crowd held rapt by their every word. Unfortunately for them, the usual crowd of teenagers in a college classroom is rarely appreciative and never rapt. Thus, schools often give their faculty members a chance to hold court before people who will actually listen, i.e., other professors. Sure, they put up posters and calendars announcing such lectures, but those go almost entirely ignored by the student body. Except for you.

You'll want to keep yourself apprised of which professor is speaking when. You need not attend every lecture, only those given by professors in whose classes you wish to improve your grade. And no—given the ever-decreasing size of headphones—you need not actually listen to most of what's being said. Just make sure not to doze off. Otherwise not only might you harm the grade you're trying to fix, but also your snoring might blacklist you among all other professors in attendance, at least one of whom you will probably have the following semester.

In addition to demonstrating your interest in the lecture simply by being in attendance, it is to your advantage to actually pay minor attention at least twice during the (inevitably) long-winded speech. It's not imperative for you to understand what's being said, especially since the only purpose of listening is to have something to ask him at the post-lecture luncheon: a simple "I didn't quite get that part about mercantilism. Would you mind quickly explaining it to me?" At which point, he will launch into a brief, thirty-six-minute bit of speechifying. Note that it's best to ask questions like this when in the company of both your professor and another faculty member, who will certainly have his own, brief treatise to synopsize in return. Having this academic buffer minimizes the chance that your professor will attempt to put the conversation back on you. And while the two teachers verbally parry and thrust, you've nothing to do but stand there and look smart.

**Attending a dean's luncheon gets you one step closer
to being on the dean's list.**

② The One-Person Greeting Committee

Aside from handing over the podium to its own teaching staff, all schools from time to time bring in outside speakers to prattle on incessantly about some bit of academic minutiae. Depending on the particular star quality of the guest, any number of faculty members will pull strings to be part of the welcoming committee, that gaggle of sycophants who exist to bask in the glow of a professor who has written a book people have actually read. With the rare exception of bona fide celebrity guests, students steer clear of this committee. That's because they don't possess the big-picture vision of the Overachieving Underperformer.

While the downside of having to spend even more time around academic types is apparent, the benefits of inflating your grade is ultimately greater. First and most instantly gratifying is the free food and drink. The bigger the guest, the better the fare. You're also working your way into the faculty inner circle, wherein you'll be privy to gossip and insider information unavailable to other students. And if you can actually manage to get some face time with the esteemed guest speaker, you'll soon find yourself being pumped for information from professors who did not get the same opportunity. The faculty will forgive your minor academic trespasses. Your fellow students will entreat you to use your influence on their behalf . . . in exchange for help with your art history paper.

Chapter 16

SYCOPHANCY IS FUN(DAMENTAL): RETYPING YOUR PROFESSORS' LECTURES AND PAPERS INTO A SPOT ON THE DEAN'S LIST

Many professors will tell their students that what they really enjoy about teaching is the thrill of debating with and being challenged by students with new, innovative ideas. These professors are lying through their teeth. In truth, most academics only enjoy defending their scholarly theses when they come out on top. Better still, professors love nothing more than knowing that they've converted a young, impressionable mind to their own way of thinking. What Overachieving Underperformers know that their professors don't is that one need not believe in what one is writing when preparing a paper.

① Conversion Factor

Fact 1: Almost all professors (certainly the tenured ones) have published articles and papers on the subjects they teach in class.

Fact 2: Some professors don't want their students to know that they haven't come up with a new idea in four decades, so these articles and papers are generally not on the required reading list.

Fact 3: A quick search online or at the library will unearth what you're looking for.

Plan of Action: Skim through what your professor has written and look for parts where she assails the teachings of other academics. Make note of their names and then begin your paper by saying something like, "While the school of thought espoused by [insert name here] is ostensibly a sound one, it falls apart when you consider. . . " Then proceed to—without naming your professor—use exactly the same points she uses in her writing. It might help to slightly misstate one of your professor's ideas. This will avail her of the opportunity to correct your minor error, thereby demonstrating her complete grasp of the topic.

Result: By attacking your professor's intellectual enemy in a method identical to her own, you build a sense of camaraderie with her. Also, so long as you agree with her completely, she'll overlook any minor logical flaws in your reasoning (since it's her reasoning to begin with).

② Number One Fan

Fact 1: In addition to articles and papers, many of your professors have published actual books.

Fact 2: Most students rarely take the time to appreciate how much work their professor has put into writing an entire textbook.

Fact 3: Like any other author, professors' egos are bruised when, at the end of the semester, they see all of their students selling these books back to the bookshop.

Plan of action: Show your appreciation. After class one day approach your professor with a starstruck blush and ask him if he would be so nice as to autograph your copy of his book. Explain that you've actually had this copy for a couple of years and that it's what piqued your interest in the subject to begin with.

Result: Your professor will be both taken aback and charmed by your request. He'll remember this moment for quite a while. So when a few weeks later you meekly ask for a two-day extension for that paper you haven't begun yet, he'll be more than happy to grant it to you. After all, how could he say no to his number one fan?

OVERACHIEVING AT UNDERPERFORMING

Find out if your professor has written a book that has nothing to do with the subject he teaches. If you ask your physics professor to sign a copy of his self-published book of poetry, you may just be able to skip class for the rest of the semester.

Be your professor's number one fan and earn that much-needed extension.

THE LEGEND OF PROFESSORS HATFIELD AND McCOY:
A STEP-BY-STEP GUIDE TO AGITATING YOUR WAY TO AN A

In academe feuding between professors is quite common, if not downright rampant. And, as is frequently the case with feuds, the underlying reason for the schism is minor and often petty. One professor emphasizes Shakespeare only in the context of Elizabethan England; the other claims that Shakespeare's writing is timeless and that focusing on historical context detracts from the value of the work. Over lesser arguments than this, blood has been shed. The Overachieving Underperformer doesn't bother himself with taking sides in such debates; he's too busy pitting one professor against the other for his own well being.

1 Professors Hatfield and McCoy have vastly different opinions on the same subject. So Steve enrolls in both of their classes.

2 **Steve listens in class for what each professor says about the other.**

3 **When it comes time for Steve to write papers, he plays directly into their mutual animosity.**

④ By taking both sides, Steve's grades improve significantly.

SECTION IV
Homework

The undergraduate Overachieving Underperformer doesn't waste all of his exploitative skills on his professors, especially since it's often much easier to employ them on his fellow students. From providing painstaking notes to editing your papers, there are countless services your peers are willing to perform for you. All you need to know is how to get it out of them. That's where this next section comes in handy.

Chapter 17

THE WEAKEST LINK:
SCORING THE EASIEST SECTION OF ANY GROUP ASSIGNMENT

Surely you've heard the old adage that a team is only as good as its worst player. Well, that's all well and good for motivating preadolescents, but in the real world of actual group dynamics it requires some revision. A professional football team isn't as good as its least-gifted athlete; that's why he sits on the bench. A band isn't judged on its least talented musician; that's why she's stuck playing the tambourine. And yet both the benchwarmer and the backup percussionist are still deemed vital parts of the functioning unit. Seen through this lens, the saying ought to be rewritten as such: A team is only as good as the people who are actually playing, but even the worst player is going to get some of the credit.

① Making the Cut: How to End Up in the Right Group

Over the years professors have devised various methods for divvying up their students into smaller groups for the purpose of some large, often long-term project. Of course, you'll want to be lumped together with as many Overachievers as possible, but that's not always something easily accomplished. What follows is a guide that you should find immensely helpful for those times when your most important task is putting together a crack squad.

The first thing you'll need to do when you receive word of an upcoming group assignment is to find out how the groups will be selected. This should be as simple as making an innocent (sounding) inquiry to your professor. Once you've got your answer, your approach varies.

ⓐ The OU Draft

On some occasions, professors will ask for volunteers to be "team leaders," someone whose initial act is to hand pick team members from the rest of the class. It goes without saying that you want to be one of these people. Thus, when your professor divulges that he plans on this form of team organization, you

---

WARNING

Do *not* be suckered into picking a good-looking student simply because of your attraction to that person. Whatever romance-in-the-library fantasies you may have stewing in your head are just that—fantasies. In the rare instance that this gorgeous coed also happens to be a dyed-in-the-wool Overachiever, you should still think twice before choosing him or her, lest you allow your attraction to keep you from letting him or her do all the work.

---

need to volunteer immediately. Explain your enthusiasm by telling your professor you're really struggling to overcome your shyness and that being pushed into a position such as team leader would do you a world of good. Once you're in front of the class picking and choosing, it shouldn't be too much of a challenge to score at least one raging Overachiever.

Choose Your Own Adventure

Students often are allowed to form teams amongst themselves. This typically results in the smartest students being drawn together into one supergroup that ends up putting everyone else's work to shame. But again, with a little early footwork, you can find your way into one of these dream teams. As soon as you know the time is drawing nigh to select groups, you need to reach out to some of the people who you'll want to carry you on their shoulders to a decent grade. Listen to the comments they make in class (especially when they are correcting or backhandedly mocking other students' lack of knowledge). After class, or when you "accidentally" run into one of them in the hallway, say something like, "Can you believe the drivel that Mitch kid was spewing? How inane! What could he possibly have been thinking? You really nailed him." By simultaneously praising the Overachiever and belittling someone he or she deems inferior, you're demonstrating that the two of you are kindred spirits. After a few minutes of conversation, whisper to your new friend that you've heard that a group assignment is coming up in the next week. Suggest that the two of you join forces with others of like mind. Thus, when the time arrives for groups to be formed, you've already got your seat booked on the Overachiever Express.

TIP Name-dropping always helps, especially if you've got an Over-achiever for a roommate. Grade grubbers are an exclusive bunch, but merely mentioning the name of one of their own could give you just enough geek cred to gain entry to their inner circle.

② Slackocracy in Action

Congratulations! You've managed to weasel your way into a group of students who—with or without your assistance—will manage to put together a final project of a higher quality than you could imagine. But how do you go from being an active part of the team to being placed on the injured reserve list?

ⓐ Start Early and with Enthusiasm!

Once the group is set and tasks have been meted out, it's time to get cracking on your portion of the project. Be enthusiastic; go overboard! If it's your job to create a computer slide show of post-World War II Vienna, tell them you plan to go the extra mile and add sound effects and movie clips. Be sure to scribble a quick yet convincing outline of what you're planning so you can show your "work" to the rest of the group. They'll swiftly remove you from that part of the project and relegate you to making sure the note cards for the presentation are placed in the correct order (which shouldn't be tough; someone else will number them for you).

ⓑ Agreeing to Disagree

Just about all college assignments involve you putting forth a viewpoint on a particular subject and defending it against critique, and group projects are no different. However, when you are dealing with teams of three or more people, dissent is not uncommon. That's why, once your group has locked into its position on the topic, you would be well served by opting to oppose, especially if all the others in the group are dead set in their unified opinion. You don't even need to have solid reasoning to back up your contrarian attitude; simply say things like, "I don't know if we're on solid ground on this one..." or, "Something just isn't adding up." Soon, the others in your group will come to realize you're never going to come around to their way of thinking (not that you even understand what it is) and that your unabashed skepticism could seep into whatever portion of the project you've been assigned to carry out. You'll quickly be taken off anything even mildly important and given control over something trivial, such as whether to use clear or multicolored index tabs for your final report.

Chapter 18

RECYCLING OLD PAPERS:
GOOD FOR THE ENVIRONMENT, GREAT FOR YOUR GPA

For most students, college is a time of activism, idealism, and faith in the notion that this generation of up-and-comers is the one that will finally put the world right. The causes are myriad and run the gamut from the global ("End world hunger!") to the peculiar ("No more chicken Kiev in the dining hall!") The vast array of political and culinary movements can be quite daunting, often to the point where students end up sitting idle, wishing to be involved but uncertain of how to choose the right cause to support. Fortunately for the Overachieving Underperformer, this is all pointless fretting. He has his cause: recycling.

Depending on your particular course of study, you could be assigned anywhere from thirty to fifty to one hundred or more papers during your college years. That's an awful lot of time, energy, and paper spent on these treatises that no one besides you and your professor (and perhaps that Nigerian guy down the hall—see Chapter 20) will ever read. Ask yourself: If your professors are going to make you jump through the same hoops over and over again, shouldn't you be allowed to do the same jump a few times? If a paper written for one professor's class is related to the material you're supposed to be learning from a second professor, what could be the harm in filling two requirements with one paper?

Great Minds Pick Classes That Are Alike

Here is another situation where a little bit of advance planning can result in a huge payout later. When you're selecting your classes for the upcoming semester, think in terms of paper recycling. Find a variety of classes (they need not be in the same department) that might cover the same topics. In the humanities you'll often find that you can spread one paper out over three or four classes. For example:

- **English Literature 254: Post-Vietnam Fiction in America**
  If you don't have one already, write a paper about the effect of America's late-70s financial woes on the country's literature.

- **Economics 202: Macroeconomics**
  Put your paper in the recycling bin and, with some changes to the introductory paragraph, you now have an essay ready to go on how the cultural climate of the time was a cause of the devastating stagflation.

- **US Government 322: The Modern President**
  Add a paragraph blaming Johnson and Nixon for good measure.

- **Film Studies 219: Portraits of War**

  If you were careful to select only books that were later made into movies, do a find-and-replace changing "literary work" to "film," and you're done!

  And while your Overachieving classmates have foregone free time to slog away on multiple papers tailored to each class, you've been hanging out with the girls they blew off so they could go to the library.

Because you haven't had to write a paper in two years, you've got plenty of time to date the girls who spurn the joyless Overachievers.

TIP It might benefit you to spread your paper recycling over the course of several semesters. It affords you the opportunity to tweak your writing based on the feedback you receive from each professor; not only will you have a paper that you can use for the next two years, but also it's going to improve each time you turn it in!

OVERACHIEVING AT UNDERPERFORMING

What about those times when you take a class assuming you'll be able to recycle a paper from your bin only to be assigned a very specific topic, one unrelated to any of your previous papers? Those Overachieving Underperformers with a little extra where it counts might be so bold as to attempt a move known as the Shoehorn.

After recovering from the devastating news that your professor's plans for your paper differ greatly from what you'd been planning to turn in, approach your professor and explain that—through a number of other classes in tangential topics—you've taken a special interest in the role of horse racing in modern culture. Admit humbly that, yes, you know it's not exactly what she wants for the assignment, but that you really think it would be very interesting to relate the topic to her subject of Picasso's post-cubist work. The worst she can do is say no.

FRIENDS WITH BENEFITS:
CHOOSING JUST THE RIGHT WORDS WHEN BORROWING SOMEONE'S NOTES

When it comes to class work, Overachievers tend to prize one item above all others: their notes, their meticulous, thorough, immaculate notes. They are what most clearly sets Overachievers apart from Underachievers, the riffraff who can never be bothered to carry a pen and who are always annoying the note-takers during lectures by inquiring, "What'd the professor just say about zinc?" As a sad consequence, prying these prized bits of classroom stenography from the clutches of an Overachiever is not easily accomplished. Traditional magic words such as "please," "pretty please," and "give me your damned notes, egghead" will do nothing but paint you as another class-skipping clod. No, this situation requires the Overachieving Underperformer's trademarked brand of verbal finesse.

It's all in the delivery. Remembering that Overachievers come in a variety of shapes, sizes, and flavors, you'll need to custom-tailor your approach. What follows is an introductory guide to charming the notes off an Overachiever.

- **The Compliment**

  For the Overachiever who's always in search of an ego stroke, try:

  "Wow...I am really impressed by how you always seem to ask just the right question in class. I bet your notes are amazing. Would you mind if I took a peek?"

- **The Flirt**

  For the Overachiever who's easily swayed by a wink, give this a shot:

  "You look really cute today. Is that a new cardigan? You want to meet up later and study? You should bring an extra copy of your notes."

- **The Medical Jargon**

  For premed students who assume that anyone who uses complex anatomical terms can't possibly be a slacker:

  "I've got a hairline fracture in my second metacarpus; might have a strain in my flexor carpi radialis, so it hurts to write.... Could I photocopy your notes?"

- **The Poem**

  For the literate Overachiever, a Haiku should help:

  Notes, well, mine are crap.
  Your notes are my salvation.
  With help, I might pass.

- **The Guilt Trip**

  For an Overachiever who feels guilty about being so much smarter than the other students:

  "I dunno... I mean, I try to take good notes, but the professors always make me feel like a second-class citizen compared to you guys [break into tears]. I... I... I just wish that I could have a set of good notes to study from for once."

- **The Campaign Promise**

  For the Overachiever who's running for student office and is lagging in the polls:

  "I can deliver one vote for every page of notes you give me."

OVERACHIEVING AT UNDERPERFORMING

Overachievers worship their notes so much that, unlike the rest of the student population, many of them keep their notebooks on their bookshelf like trophies long after a class is over. So your best bet may be to go hunting around your dorm for these stellar students and their prized work. Unlike the Overachievers currently taking the class, these Overachievers have nothing to gain by shutting you out, and it will be a huge ego stroke to them when you tell them how you heard about their legendary note taking skills.

Chapter 19

"Was I Not Supposed to Mix Those?"
aka Being the Bad Lab Partner

There are those who believe there is a balance to nature, that for every positive thing there exists something negative to even it out. Furthermore, there are those who believe that this good/bad split is necessary, lest the planet be thrown off its axis and into oblivion. Whatever the veracity of this school of thought, it's wise for the Overachieving Underperformer to be mindful of this paradigm when stuck in a lab class. The worse your work is, the better your lab partner has to perform in order for you both to pass.

Generally speaking, there are two phases to almost any lab project: The experiment and the write-up. Herewith, methods for doing as little as possible on both.

① Ooops! Explosive Behavior

When you were a child and had a potentially dangerous toy, what was the fastest way to compel your parents to wrest it from your hands? By allowing said toy to live up to its potential. Whether it was shooting your sister in the leg with a BB gun or spearing your uncle's hand with a lawn dart, the implement of destruction was locked away or in the trash before you could scream, "Unfair!" The same holds true for working with a lab partner. The faster you can cause a minor disaster, the faster you can get back to being the one who just has to stand there and look busy.

You might not even have to take it to the point of doing damage. There are some ways to get your lab partner to take over before things even get started:

ⓐ The Shakes: If the experiment involves the handling of caustic chemicals or the precise cutting of materials, it's to your advantage to have hands that tremble so badly you'd be hard-pressed to hold a pencil, let alone something lethal. If your partner allows your vibrating fingers to venture anywhere near that beaker full of sulfuric acid, either he is a sadist or he's lazier than you.

ⓑ Slapstick Sidekick: Every good comedy duo has the guy who manages to break everything within his vicinity. When you introduce yourself to your lab partner, shake his hand and then "accidentally" fall to the floor, bringing him with you. In class, every time you get something out of your bag, don't just drop it on the ground, find a way to scatter all of your belongings everywhere. And since a science lab isn't exactly the ideal setting for wacky physical comedy, your lab partner will do whatever he can to prevent you from being anywhere within five miles of the experiment.

If neither of these manages to beguile your partner into preempting you from working on the experiment, here are some things you can do once the Bunsen burner's been lit:

ⓒ Losing Contact: To complete an experiment with any success requires a modicum of precision and care. If you've "lost a contact lens" and your vision is so bad that you can't manage to pour liquid from one beaker into another without spilling every drop, you've no business wearing a lab coat. So . . . walk into stools, desks, and your partner. Whatever is required to convince him of your impaired vision.

ⓓ The Devil's Grin: It's one thing to enjoy working in a lab. It's another to get psychotically revved up by it. When you light the Bunsen burner, turn the flame up as high as it can go and stare into it, grinning salaciously; lick your lips if you like. If the experiment requires potent solvents, start raving to your partner about all the cool stuff you could melt with it, and then start wondering aloud where you could get your hands on mass quantities of it. But be careful: You want your partner to take over all the work, not call the FBI on you.

Get *out* of lab work by getting too *into* your lab work.

② I Writes Good. You Write with Considerably Superior Adroitness.

After the in-lab portion of the experiment is completed (by your partner), it's time to move on to getting your partner to put your findings into words. Since your only contribution thus far has been to stand clear of all things flammable, chances are, your partner will attempt to hornswoggle you into being the one responsible for the write-up. Again, there are a couple of proactive steps you can take to prevent it from ever getting to that stage:

ⓐ **Kid's Play:** While the lab portion of the assignment is still in progress and your partner is attempting to keep you at arm's length, take the opportunity to regress to the inquisitive days of your childhood. Discuss every minute detail of what's going on: "What kind of fuel do you think the burner uses?" "I wonder what makes Pyrex so much better than other glass." "Why does water bubble when you boil it?" After a few hours of demonstrating that you have no command over basic science, your lab partner wouldn't dream of allowing someone so clueless mangle the work he's done with an idiotic write-up.

ⓑ **Coin a Phrase:** In your discussions with your lab partner don't feel obligated to stay within the stuffy confines of proper English, or any language for that matter. Unrestrain yourself and constructify whatever new words and phrases your wishtitude desireates. If your lab partner still gives you the go-ahead to pen the write-up, you might want to think about dropping the class.

TIP As has been mentioned earlier, Overachievers tend to run in tight packs. Unfortunately for you, this means that, by being the bad lab partner, you risk word of your ineptness getting around to other people whose help you might need at a later time. Thus, it behooves you to select a lab partner who is not only an Overachiever, but who is also a recluse. The fewer friends your partner has, the fewer people he can tell about being saddled with a moron in his organic chemistry lab.

Chapter 20

PARENTAL GUIDANCE: DOING YOUR BEST
(TO CONVINCE YOUR PARENTS THAT A B- IS A STELLAR GRADE)

The fact that an overwhelming majority of college students receive some, if not all, of their financial support from their parents is a double-edged sword. Although, yes, it is certainly better to have someone else footing the bill for all of your full-time fun and occasional education, this endowment often does not come without recompense. Even if they're also college graduates (and thus able to empathize with your plight), your parents will not be satisfied with a mediocre return on their investment. This leaves you with two options. First, you can burn the candle at both ends and eschew any notion of enjoying the college experience. Or you could use some of the following techniques for getting Mom and Dad to believe you really are trying to succeed.

❶ Grade Deflation

Beginning in the latter portion of the twentieth century, a large number of colleges initiated (often unofficial) policies of what was to become known as "grade inflation." This term refers to a college's artificially raising the general level of its students' grades. Many parents and educators raised their voices in complaint over this growing phenomenon. However, grade inflation continues to be practiced on a large scale. And this fact works to your advantage.

If your parents complain about your last set of marks (way to go—all B-s!), explain to them that your school actually believes in "grade deflation," wherein they set up higher than normal limits. Tell them that what is an A at most schools is only a B+ at your school. Hopefully, you've got a cousin in a different college who's outperforming you academically. So when your parents point out that cousin Sean is getting straight As at his school, explain that they've just proved your point. There's no way Sean is that much smarter than you, right?

❷ Displacing Blame

Blaming one's parents for one's woes is a tried and true tradition. You didn't ask to be born, so why should you be held responsible for how poorly you're doing in school? Tell them how the pressure they put on you to succeed is only succeeding at pushing you toward failure. If, when you were deciding on colleges, they nudged you even slightly in the direction of your current school, remind them that you "never wanted to go this stupid college anyway!" If you had just been able to go to that other school that cost a little more and was a little farther away, things would have been different.

TIP If your parents force you to transfer schools because of slipping grades, you can always exploit this forced uprooting for even more reason to blame your parents for poor grades in the future.

③ Sob Story

There's a way to make your parents feel guilty about your grades that doesn't involve pointing the finger at them directly: Point the finger at yourself. Have a mini-breakdown. Fake apologize to them in a sincere and self-loathing manner. Put all the blame on your young shoulders. Admit that your parents have wasted so much money on you and you've been a horrible child. Tell them your embarrassment at having done so poorly is why you never call them anymore: You're ashamed. Be "honest" and say you want to keep trying—you know you're almost there—but that you wouldn't hate them if they pulled you from school now and put you to work pulling weeds in the back yard.

**Blame all of your failure on yourself and
it will miraculously transfer to your parents.**

All of this weeping and self-flagellation should have the desired effect of engendering in your parents a belief that perhaps they, not you, are to blame for your middling academic performance. In the worst possible world, they'd pull you out of school for a semester and you'd all end up in family counseling. Most likely, rather than dealing with their possible role in your neuroses, they'll put a few bucks in your pocket and send you back to school.

WARNING

If you're going to pull the Sob Story, be careful not to sound sarcastic or facetious when blaming yourself. If your parents get a whiff of your fakery, they might just take you up on your offer to leave school forever.

INTERNATIONAL TRADE:
THE BENEFITS OF FRACTURED-ENGLISH-SPEAKING FRIENDS

Most colleges provide students with the unique opportunity to meet students from around the country and around the world. International scholars bring with them knowledge and expertise in any number of fields, but for many of them the tricky particulars of the English language prove to be a stumbling block. Luckily, you speak English, and speak it good.

For a student of French history, detailing Napoleon's defeat at the Battle of Leipzig shouldn't require any more effort than the act of tying one's shoes. But being forced to provide these details in a language that one is still adjusting to is undoubtedly difficult. A slip-up of a sentence—such as, "President McKinley were assassinated in 1901"—appears amateurish to any one of us, but the mistake is easy enough to make if English is still a foreign language to you. Thus, you, as someone with a decent enough grasp on the language to be reading a book, should seek out the international students and offer tutoring and assistance wherever necessary.

Before you begin wondering what ulterior motive lies hidden in this bit of charity, consider the following: Most international students come here because their fields of study are in the sciences and engineering. So while conjugating the verb "to run" might be a tough one for them, calculating the volume of an irregular solid is second nature. The trade-off is obvious: While you're "helping" him by correcting "Amundsen finded the South Pole in 1911," your new friend from Turkmenistan is correcting your calculus homework. You're both going to do well on your respective assignments, but really, it's clear which party does better in the end on this exchange.

SECTION V
Advanced Studies

With everything you've learned thus far, you should be able to make it through your college career with little trouble and graduate with respectable marks to the delight of your smiling parents. That being said, there is always more that can be done to do less. For example, who says you can't skip classes all year long? Or that you should complete your degree within the standard time frame? And why should you stick to blowing off work in your own country when you've got an entire world waiting for you to ask for an extension on your paper?

Chapter 21

CORRUPTING THE INTELLIGENTSIA OF TOMORROW:
BEING A TEACHER'S ASSISTANT

Getting older is not without its perks. Take, for an example, the phenom-enon of the teacher's assistant. Most colleges have several large (often required) classes that have too many students on the roster to make any one-on-one time with the professor possible. As a solution, the mass of students is subdivided into more manageable groups run not by professors or assistant professors, but by graduate students and, sometimes, senior undergraduates. Aside from the automatic credits and letters of recommendation doing this work merits you, it's also possible to exploit your youthful charges for your own benefit.

① The Assistants to the Assistant

Given that your average teacher's assistant (TA) is responsible for a dozen or so students, it's all but guaranteed that your group will include at least one nestling Overachiever. The beauty of someone so young and so eager to make a positive impression is that they're still naïve enough to buy whatever you're selling, so long as it's sold with authority. Remember this when you find yourself in the unusual position of having to do research. It's time to pass the buck to the kid who wants it most. At the beginning of one of your sessions, announce that the professor has "a ton" of research that he needs done for his next book. The "professor" has asked that each TA recommend one student to help out. Of course, there isn't a kernel of truth to any of this, but your little Overachiever is honing his library skills (not to mention building up his lower-back muscles with all those extra books) while you've managed to get all the prep work done on your thesis without having to lift a finger.

② Students Teaching Students

Okay, so you've gotten out of having to take a real class by "teaching" a discussion section to a bunch of freshmen. And you've gotten one of your students to do all of your research for your thesis credits. However, you have yet to get out of having to occasionally teach a lesson to your charges. Fear not; help is on the way.

In the name of developing your students' presentation skills, start a system whereby each of your students in the discussion group takes turns giving a fifteen-minute recap of the professor's lecture. After that, open up the remainder of the hour to questions and comments from the other students. Tell the students that you are grading them on classroom participation, so shrinking violets beware. If you've got yourself a couple of verbose Overachievers, you might never have to say anything for the rest of the semester save, "Who's turn is it today?"

Get the students to teach themselves and put your semester on cruise control.

OVERACHIEVING AT UNDERPERFORMING

At the end of each semester, students are usually required to fill out evaluation forms for their professors and TAs. And while most TA positions are not graded, the student evaluations do become part of your file that professors use when writing letters of reference for graduate schools and jobs. Thus, it's in your best interest to have students who both liked the way you ran the class and are convinced that you have some say in their final grades.

In the classes leading up to the evaluation, bring up horror stories you've "heard from someone" about how some of the other TAs are running their sections. "I heard if you talk out of turn in Roberta's section, she makes you do push-ups." "Gordon makes fun of everyone's outfits . . . and God help you if you're overweight." After being privy to these bits of propaganda, your students will write you a glowing review.

As they're filling out the evaluations you should also drop little "I'm joking" hints such as, "Hey, you guys are aware that I can identify everyone's handwriting?" and, "Before you fill in that 'poor' box, Jill, you might want to remember that time you didn't come to class for, what was it called . . . November?" Suddenly, you've instilled a twinge of fear in them that you might alter their grades if they mess with your chances of getting accepted to grad school.

Chapter 22

THE RUN-ON LIFE SENTENCE:
PUTTING THAT FIVE-, SIX-, OR SEVEN-YEAR PLAN INTO ACTION

For most people, college marks a high-water mark in their life. You're no longer an awkward adolescent. You're free from the shackles of constant parental supervision. You're meeting like-minded people from other parts of the world. Everything seems to be on the upswing. As an Overachieving Underperformer, you're doing even better because you've managed both decent grades and a fulfilling social life. The only down side of your time in college is that it eventually has to end. Or does it?

1. The Virtue of Thrift

College is fun. That's why it costs so much money. Most people would stay in college a lot longer than they do if they could manage the financial strain. If your ultimate goal is to be in college so long that you'll need two hands to count the years, it helps to select the least expensive school you can find (and that fits the criteria set out in Chapter 27). Additionally, most extremely affordable colleges are located in affordable areas, bringing down your cost of living in general. So if your parents are going to foot the bill, they're less apt to freak out if your dillydallying isn't eating into their wallet.

2. Major Changes

One strategy for implementing an extended-year plan is to keep changing the direction of your scholarly path. From physics to sociology to history to library sciences, you should get as close to completing a major as possible before changing horses and heading off in a different direction. If at any moment you decide it's time to finally leave campus, simply finish off one of your several fields of study and voila! You've got a degree.

TIP If your university comprises several different specialized schools, consider the benefits of a transfer. Since each school probably has its own set of required classes, a transfer from, say, the engineering school to the business school means that you're all but starting from scratch.

3. The Part-Time is the Right Time

The easiest way to live a longer college life is to switch into part-time mode, where you're only paying for the classes you take and you can take them at your leisure. If needed, you can pick up a part-time job to match your education. Schools often have no limit to the number of years part-time students can continue attending classes. It's possible

MARINE BIOLOGY

PHYSICS

JOURNALISM

MATH

Don't let tradition keep you from finding your true inner academic.
Change majors as often as you wish, and stay in school for however long you desire.

that by the time you ultimately get your degree, you'll be standing on the platform next to your grandchildren.

Learn how to combine part-time learning and part-time working and you'll be the coolest senior (citizen) on campus.

TIP Your decision to lead the part-time life will inevitably ruffle some people's feathers. Your parents and advisers will be disappointed and assume that you secretly want to drop out of school. Explain to them how important you feel it is not to lose touch with the real world and that the ivory tower world of college is slowly numbing you to the harsh truths of adult life. Tell them you have no intention of dropping out; in fact, all this soul-searching has convinced you that you should transfer into the nursing program.

Chapter 23

SUMMER SESSION:
WASTING YOUR PARENTS' MONEY ALL YEAR ROUND

One of the reasons college life is so appealing is the fact that no matter how difficult or simple your course of study, you rarely have to study continuously for an entire calendar year. Many students look forward to the respite that the summer months bring: sleeping until noon with impunity, free home cooking and laundry, seeing friends and family. True, there is usually the yoke of parental proximity around one's neck, but freedom from the burdens of the academic year is often worth the filial pains.

But think about what you're giving up: Since the Overachieving Underperformer's semester isn't terribly taxing to begin with, you should ask yourself, *Why should I take a break from taking a break?*

Of course, fun rarely comes without a price tag, and taking summer classes is no exception. You're going to need to convince the folks to ante up the requisite cash. Here are some methods worth trying if you desire a deep, rich academic tan.

WARNING

Prying open the parental purse is difficult enough without the truth interfering. Whatever you tell your family, do not mention that your main reason for not coming home is to avoid them.

1 The Turnaround

As previously mentioned, parents often assume you could be doing better. If you want to get them to pay for a few summer classes (and the other associated costs of living), you might want to tell them they're right. Explain to them that you're ashamed at how you've been doing up to this point and that you feel it's time to "turn things around." Then tell them you know what would really help you get back into the academic swing of things—taking a couple of classes this summer. After all, you won't have all the social distractions that plagued you all year long, right? And with only a couple classes to focus on, you should be able to live up to that neglected potential. Of course, since you won't get your grades from the summer session until your parents have already paid for the next full semester, how you perform really won't matter.

TIP Take some classes that you actually can ace without much effort. It will give you some leverage on your overall average, and after your grades fall again during the regular year, your parents will be prone to believing that summer time is the right time next year, too.

② The (Invisible) Internship

There are some chances that only come along once in a lifetime, like assisting a professor on a summer project. Explain to your parents that only three students get chosen for this special honor and that you'd be

stupid not to accept the offer. And since you'd only be working in the afternoons, you'd be even stupider not to take a morning class or two to fill in the rest of the day. This is all a lie, but, c'mon, are your parents really going to check? Of course not. If you're lucky, they'll opt against paying for any summer classes, not out of thrift but because they don't want any extra work interfering with your "internship," which consists of sipping iced tea in an air-conditioned room paid for by Mom and Dad.

Chapter 24

INTERNSHIPS:
FOOLING PEOPLE WITH REAL JOBS INTO GIVING YOU A REFERENCE

Many companies (certainly most large corporations) offer internships to college students, some during the academic year, many that run between terms. It's a bit of a one-sided proposition. The companies are supplied with an army of eager, fresh-faced—and, most important, unpaid—temporary labor. The interns get real-life office experience like filing and having to wake up before sunrise to commute. And all for no money. Overachievers fall into the intern trap because they see it as a chance to get a sliver of a toenail in the door for a real job later. But as we've already seen, Overachievers are collectively a bunch of suckers. What sets Overachieving Underperformers apart from the rest of the pack is their ability to mine even the most unpleasant situation for their own profit. Here are some ways to reap the benefits of internships while skipping out on all of the busy work that is usually part of the package.

① The Buddy System

Generally speaking, interns are free agents to be used for whatever purpose by whomever. Even in companies where interns rotate from department to department, the work remains just about the same. Filing for someone in the legal department is really no different from filing for someone in accounting. Another universal fact is that there's always someone who feels bad giving the interns so much to do in exchange for so little. You need to find this person, aka the Intern's Buddy and stick to her like green on grass.

But how to identify a Buddy? It's often quite simple, because office workers tend to descend upon new interns like vultures on a fresh carcass. Within your first day, you'll field requests ranging from "get me coffee" to "get me a latte" from just about everyone. Between runs to the coffee shop, take your time and look around the office. Seek out the people who haven't bothered you, those who have managed to procure their own caffeinated beverages. Take a second and introduce yourself to them. With tongue planted firmly in cheek, tell them you're available to file something or shine their shoes, sweep their chimney, polish their silverware, trim their hedges, and mow their lawns if needed. This good-natured icebreaker, if executed correctly, should lay the groundwork for you and your Buddy.

Once you've located your Buddy, it's time to use this temporary relationship to your advantage. Whenever you're not working (which will gradually become more and more often), take as many opportunities as possible to stop in and chat. Find out whom they dislike and who, if anyone, is like-minded in their approach to interns. Make sure you discuss it with your Buddy if one of her foes asks you to do some tiresome task. Feel free to just come out and tell her, "Jeez, everyone else treats me so badly. I wish I could just work for you all the

A good Intern Buddy will shield you from having to toil in the office.

time." At worst, your Buddy will come up with things for you to do to keep you out of the clutches of others. At best, your Buddy will begin covering for you, telling her coworkers that you're unavailable because she has you working on something special.

② Casual Fridays

Just as office workers pounce on new interns like kittens to catnip when it comes to doing unpleasant busy work, they are often just as eager to try to make some sort of social connection with the cool college kids. You are often an injection of youthful exuberance into a socially stale workplace. Many of the same people who have you running around chasing your tail all day will invite you out on the town at night, especially if your internship is in a city that you've never lived in or visited. They will try to impress you with their hipness by name-dropping their favorite bands. Or they might demonstrate how worldly and urbane they are by getting you past the doorman at a trendy nightspot. They'll mostly want to introduce you to what they consider fun: sitting in a bar after work with the same people you've been around all day at work. Regardless, it benefits your future to venture out and about with these folks.

It's very rare that office workers remember those interns who filed the fastest or who distributed memos most thoroughly. They do, however, remember that intern who told that dirty joke that made Parker from inventory spit beer all over Shirley from purchasing, or that intern who brought down the house with his karaoke rendition of "Copacabana." These are memories that last—while maybe not a lifetime, at least long enough for you to ask these people for a reference a few months later. And since every intern (in spite of the quality or quantity of work done) gets at least a decent reference, these coworkers will give you praise worthy of someone who actually did something during his three-month internship.

SEMESTER ABROAD:
WHAT HAPPENS IN COPENHAGEN STAYS IN COPENHAGEN

Almost all colleges offer opportunities for their students to spend a summer or a semester at a partner school in another country. Call it a cultural exchange or call it a global education—whatever moniker you affix to your time out of the country, it's an opportunity for you to earn college credits without having to see the same old faces for a few months. But where to go? Each destination has its own unique opportunities for enrichment. For anyone considering crossing academic borders, here's a brief guide on the whys and wherefores of your international options.

	Pros	Cons
Germany	• Oktoberfest • Girls named Greta	• No November-through-September Fest • Men named Greta
France	• Wine and cheese • Nubile, nude sunbathers on the Riviera	• Having a waiter spit in your wine • Not so nubile, but just as nude sunbathers on the Riviera
Italy	• Food, food, and more food • Good, wholesome Catholic girls	• Can't find a decent pizza to save your life • Formerly good, wholesome Catholic girls who didn't get that the marriage proposal was only an innocent joke

	Pros	**Cons**
Australia	• Drinking all day on the beach • Surfing all day at the beach	• Sharks • You will eventually have to come home
The Netherlands	• Um, well . . . the bakeries • Window shopping in the Red Light District	• Having a few too many brownies and blacking out for a week in the Red Light District • Not being able to show your parents a single photograph from your semester
Semester at Sea	• Visiting ports of call in multiple nations • Cohabitating in close quarters with coeds	• Having to learn to say "Where is the bathroom?" in twenty languages • Cohabitating in close quarters with a coed whom you don't like anymore

SECTION VI
Academia ad Eternum:
Graduate School and Beyond

Imagine extending your college life not just for a few years, or even a decade, but for the rest of your life. Think about being paid to appear to study and then being paid even more to barely teach. For an Overachieving Underperformer, it's not such a bad existence. These last chapters will lead you through the entire process, from picking which type of graduate degree to shoot for to brown nosing your way into a teaching position. It's your guide to avoiding reality for the rest of your days.

Chapter 25

Stretching Exercises: Choosing Between a Master's or a PhD ... or Both

For most academic areas, there are two levels of study beyond your undergraduate degree: a master's degree and a doctorate. Each has its own pluses and minuses, so before you go applying to graduate programs, there are some questions you'll need to ask yourself: Just how long do you plan on stretching out this whole learning process? And if you do see a terminus to your academic career, what do you expect to do when the ride comes to its end?

① Master the Possibilities

For the most part, much of the work that goes into earning a master's degree greatly resembles the work you've already done as an undergraduate. You go to classes, write papers, and take tests, just as you've already done for four (or more) years. The only real difference in the classroom is that the entirety of your focus is on one narrow subject—one that you probably lost interest in before you finished your bachelor's degree. Additionally, since you'll probably be working your way through graduate school by being a teaching assistant for undergraduate classes, it will often feel like you're reliving all the worst parts of your college life (the academics).

The main component setting a master's program apart from an undergraduate degree is the final thesis. The particulars vary, but the master's thesis is generally an original paper or project demonstrating your unique grasp (or "mastery" . . . get it?) of the topic. Some programs allow you extra time after your graduate classes are completed to finish your thesis while others expect you to complete all the work at the same time.

Getting your master's degree can be a huge drain on your fun time. Depressing matters further is the fact that in this day and age having a master's no longer guarantees you a good job or higher pay in most fields. So while you've been banging your head against the library wall, that guy Bob, whom you graduated college with but who went straight to work, will be your boss when you finally do get a job.

The best chance of being happy as a master's degree student is to make a lifestyle of it. Don't stop at one master's degree: Get five of them! If your first master's is in American literature, move on to comparative literature, then a degree in folklore studies, and another in rhetoric and communications, which can certainly be recycled into a master's in journalism with a little effort (*very* little). And there's no need to stop with five. So long as schools are willing to accept you into a program (and are willing to give you money for being there—see Chapter 27), you can keep going until you decide to get yourself into a real job—or on a TV quiz show, where you'll rake in the cash thanks to your diverse education!

A single master's degree just means you've wasted a couple of years and probably racked up more student loans.

Keep jumping from one master's program to another and you can avoid reality until you cash in as a quiz show champ.

② Doctorate Feelgood

Building on a master's degree, a doctorate requires that you write a longer, more complex thesis. Thus, you are often allowed a significant amount of time between finishing your classes and handing over your heavily researched tome for review. This means more free time for you, especially if you've managed to wangle some well-intentioned foundation out of grant money for your research into the waste disposal practices of Dutch settlers.

The most important thing about earning the doctorate notch on your belt is that it is the doorway to a life in academics. A master's degree will only get you a teaching position in a few, select areas. For the most part, if you want to see some overachieving teenager raise his hand and beg for your attention—calling you "Professor! Professor!"—you'll need to get your hands on that doctorate. Once you're in the door with that bit of parchment, you've crossed over forever from the student's world, where learning requires money, to the professor's world, where learning *earns* money. It's not a bad neighborhood in which to live.

TIP Even if you intend on getting your PhD straight from getting your bachelor's degree, you might want to look into programs that offer students the option of doing a master's program first before plunging into the doctoral depths. This way, you're guaranteed to get out of there with at least one graduate degree, but when that's over you have some choices available to you. You can just go straight on and finagle your way to the PhD, or you could switch schools and get your PhD elsewhere, or you could make a change and enter a completely different master's program in your current school or another. The academic world is your oyster!

Chapter 26

REMEMBER ME?: CONVINCING YOUR FORMER PROFESSORS THAT YOU DESERVE A RECOMMENDATION

Of the ordeals associated with applying to graduate school, perhaps the most trying is hunting around for letters of recommendation from former professors. Many students will have to poke through every inch of gray matter in their brains to come up with the names of three professors who might remember having taught them, let alone have anything positive to say about their development as students. And to the unschooled outsider, it would seem that an Overachieving Underperformer would face even greater difficulties. However, as you'll soon see, all of those years of scheming, plotting, and boondoggling will not have been in vain. If anything, you're in a better position than most of your fellow students.

Every year as application deadlines draw nigh, college professors are inundated with requests from former students—many of whom have been out in the real world for several years—for letters of recommendation. With the exception of the very best (who merit worshipful epistles) and the very worst (whose requests are summarily hurled into the recycling bin), the professors' responses tend to take on a generic "Bob was a solid B+ student in my class" variety of blah. The question facing you is, how do you get a unique and glowing recommendation when your grades were no better or worse than anyone else's?

① Getting Better All the Time

You've already seen how gradually improving the quality of your work over the course of a single term can earn you a higher grade (see Chapter 13). So why stop at one semester? Why not take the same approach to your whole undergraduate experience? Find a professor in whose course you managed a particularly effective bit of bootstrapping. If you're still in school, take some time and pay him a visit. Tell him you remember that moment in his class when you finally started to "get it." Explain that you're asking for his honest recommendation because he's seen that you have the mettle required to succeed in the face of adversity. Make sure he knows that were it not for his class—and more

---

WARNING

Although it's essentially what you're doing, never *appear* to be asking your professor to gloss over the truth about your academic record. In all your recommendation requests, make it clear that you're looking for "honesty" from your professors. The job is simply planting in their heads what your particular idea of the "truth" is.

---

importantly, him—you would not have decided to stay in school and graduate. And here you are applying to grad schools! Congratulations, you've just gotten one great letter to send off to the admissions board.

② Dragon Lady II: Return to the Lair

Supposing that you took the risk of enrolling in a course taught by the Dragon Lady (see Chapter 9), your second positive letter of recommendation could lie deep within the cave of her office. Well, it's time to go spelunking. After all, this is a professor who normally only gets requests from the small cadre of Overachievers who aced her course. Devoid of all pride, approach her and say you're well aware that your grade in her class was not stellar, but it's a B that you're exceptionally proud of because you *earned* it. Say to her that you have no delusions about being a genius but her class instilled in you a lust for learning. At this early stage in your love affair with academia, to run away and be shackled with the diurnal horrors of office work... well, that just wouldn't be right. Your direct appeal to her scholarly tendencies should mean you're walking out of her office with a brilliant letter in your hand.

③ When I Grow Up . . .

Perhaps the easiest way to get into grad school is by following directly in the path of your professor. As has already been established, professors don't generally mind being brown nosed (see Chapter 16), so there's no real reason to stop the sycophancy once that particular course is finished. Seek out the professor who most appreciated your retyping of his old papers. Tell him the good news—that you really want to take up the mantle of his specific petty academic cause by going out into the tough world of graduate school and being his apostle. If his topic isn't directly linked to the graduate programs to which you're applying, make it fit. Tell him you want to apply his views of fiscal policy

Play up your professor's pro-academia/anti-corporate tendencies and you're that much closer to a glowing letter of recommendation.

to interior design. (And don't be shocked if he already has some ideas on that far-fetched topic.) Regardless, your continued, ardent interest in his specialized field, combined with your innovative interdisciplinary notions, should earn you a letter good enough to get into at least one grad school that you don't deserve to attend.

Chapter 27

"No Stipend? No Way!":
Why You Should Never Pay for a Higher Education

How often have you heard someone say, "You get what you pay for"? The expression is generally used to imply that if one desires a quality result, one should invest a little more in a quality product. Although that adage may apply to purchasing a new toaster, when it comes to graduate school, the Overachieving Underperformer sees things in a slightly different light. The axiom still holds true—you do actually get what you pay for—but he adds the following: If you can find a school to accept you free of charge, how much work could you really be expected to do?

① Being Taken for Granted

Many graduate programs receive huge research grants from interests in both the public and private sectors. Much of this money goes to building additions to faculty members' houses, some is spent on equipment and materials, and a very small portion is used to pay graduate students a (barely) living wage. Getting your hands on some of this cash is not the easiest task. The schools with the largest endowments are often the schools with the most stringent admissions standards. Your best chance is to find a graduate program at a school ranked slightly lower than your undergraduate college. The admissions board will look at your average grades from the "better" school and be more than glad to have you aboard. And since these lower-tier schools don't have the cachet or elitist aura that draws the best students to the well-funded universities, they will throw money at you to lure you away to their "developing" program.

② "Working" for a Living

In some fields of study—and this is especially true of the arts—the number of graduate students greatly outnumbers the amount of grant money to be meted out. Only a select few students will be offered gratis educations, and any number of the professor-manipulating machinations discussed earlier could help you get your name on the short list for this funding. However, even if you are unable to suckle from the free-money teat, all hope is not lost. There is always the omnipresent oxymoron: work study.

Work study is intended as a way for graduate students to barter their services in exchange for a cheap education. Two standard forms of work-study employment have already been covered in earlier chapters—working in the library (see Chapter 5) and being a teaching assistant (see Chapter 21). But there are a couple of other jobs that you might be required to perform.

- *Research Assistant:* In addition to teaching assistants, many professors need research assistants, essentially another term for gofers and stenographers. However, these positions are also good opportunities to get to know a professor as a potential equal, which may come in handy when defending your thesis or applying for an adjunct professor position (see Chapter 28).

- *Office Work:* Here is where they throw you into the department's administrative office for a few hours a week so you can file and do some basic data entry. While it seems like the lowest of the work-study job offerings, it actually offers you an unparalleled amount of influence amongst both your fellow students, who will volunteer to copyedit the latest draft of your thesis in exchange for a peek at their personal/confidential files, and your professors, who will look upon you favorably when you're able to cut through the red tape and procure a free lecture hall or slide projector for them.

Don't underestimate the hidden benefits of a work-study job in your department's administrative office. He who controls information controls power.

Chapter 28

PUBLISH OR PERISH (AND HAVE TO GET A REAL JOB):
TURNING THAT THESIS YOU BARELY WROTE INTO A CAREER IN ACADEMIA

If you can manage the funding issues, there's really no limit to how long you can continue to amass graduate degrees. However, odds are that at some point before you die you're going to have to stop being a student. When this tidal shift occurs, you'll find yourself with two options—putting together a résumé and scouring the want ads for a real job, where you'll be starting from scratch in an alien environment, or hunting for a teaching position, where you can do exactly what you've been doing for all of your adolescent and adult life: as little as possible. For the Overachieving Underperformer, the choice is clear.

① Getting a Head Start

If you want to demonstrate that you're made of the right professorial stuff, you might want to take the initiative and ask the chair of your department if you can start a class of your own. Make it a weekly survey covering a variety of topics in your field. And instead of having to go through the arduous task of crafting a new lecture each week, invite all of the professors in your department to speak at least once. All you have to do is write a brief introduction to each professor (culled from the author bio on the back of their latest book). You'll impress the faculty members with the wide scope of your vision, and you won't upset the more leery professors by stepping on their toes. When the semester is over, collect all of the professors' lectures (with your insightful introductions) and sell the idea to some small academic publisher. Before you've even finished your doctorate, you've already managed to compose the seminal text on your topic. If that doesn't get you an assistant professorship at some college, nothing will.

OVERACHIEVING AT UNDERPERFORMING

Instead of taking the book idea directly to the publishing house yourself, consider pitching the idea to the most esteemed member of your department. Tell her she can take primary author credit, so long as you receive a coauthor credit. This will guarantee that the book gets published while also increasing the chances that someone aside from your mother might purchase it.

② Stirring the Pot

The easiest yet riskiest way to gain notoriety in academic circles is to create controversy. And the best way for a doctoral student to stir things up is to create a thesis project so outlandish that people—

academics and laymen alike—feel compelled to talk about it. If you can even semiconvincingly write a paper saying you believe Hamlet was written by a twelve-year-old boy, go for it. If you can find anything to support your outlandish theory that the 1969 moon landing actually occurred in 1954, and on Jupiter, it's your duty as an Overachieving Underperformer to document it. The only difference between a doctoral thesis and the cover story of a supermarket tabloid is the quality of writing. Here are some sample topics for you to consider assaying:

ECONOMICS
"Eat the Poor"

GOVERNMENT
"Rock-Paper-Scissors: The Right Method for Electing the President"

LITERATURE
"This Kind of Thing Never Happens to Me:
A Formalist Critique of *Penthouse's Hottest Letters, 1978-1981*"

HISTORY
"King George III: England's Secretly Female Monarch"

ART
"'Dogs Playing Poker'—Best Painting Ever"

THEATER
"In Defense of David Hasselhoff"

PHYSICS
"Gravity is for Losers"

The fact is that controversy generates publicity for a college. Publicity for a college generates student interest, which translates into higher enrollment numbers and more money. So an outrageous thesis paper, such as the one you wrote theorizing that South Dakota doesn't exist, can only benefit (at least in the short run) the small college that hires you for your first lecturing position.

Publish a controversial thesis paper and cross over the threshold into the world of the professional academic.

Just look at them go, you say to yourself while resting in the comforting shade of an aging elm tree in the middle of campus. Knowing what you do now, you feel a twinge of pity as you watch your fellow students scurry to and fro. Whether they're working themselves into the ground and missing out on what should be the best years of their life or shortsightedly tossing their futures into the gutter like an errant Frisbee, it's as if they all exist in a separate universe from yours, one where success is not attainable without the sacrifice of leisure and acting one's age is a mortal sin. But you, as an Overachieving Underperformer, have taken that next evolutionary step and transcended the simplistic labels of "studious" and "stupid." Yours is a life you could never have envisioned before and one you dare not give up now.

Be forewarned: Although you might feel pity for the go-getters and the slackers alike, they are both necessary elements to your success. As such, they cannot be let in on your secrets. Like a gifted magician, all your power rests in your ability to maintain the illusion by distraction and dexterity. Making a college degree appear out of thin air isn't impressive if everyone knows exactly how you did it.

So as the other students live and die by the clock, you now know that your time truly belongs to you alone. There's no silly rushing to a morning class, and there's no sitting in a stuffy lecture hall on a glorious spring day when you'd be much better served by spending the afternoon outside. Summer classes and part-time study mean that there's no definitive terminus to your school year, and the existence of graduate school opens the door to academic infinitude. All that remains for you to do is sit back and let others carry you through.